NAVAL RETIRING BOARD.

SPEECH

OF

HON. SAM HOUSTON, OF TEXAS,

DELIVERED

IN THE SENATE OF THE UNITED STATES, MARCH 18, 1856.

WASHINGTON:
PRINTED AT THE CONGRESSIONAL GLOBE OFFICE.
1856.

NAVAL RETIRING BOARD.

Mr. HOUSTON. Mr. President, I hold in my hand a memorial, signed unofficially by members of the Legislature of the State of Maryland. It is an indorsement of the resolutions adopted by the Legislature of Virginia some time since. I ask that they may be read; and then I design to offer some explanatory remarks, giving the reasons for my concurrence with the sentiments of the resolutions.

The Secretary read the resolutions of the Legislature of Virginia, as follows:

1. *Resolved*, As the opinion of the General Assembly of Virginia, that the action of the late naval board appointed "to promote the efficiency" of the Navy, by which two hundred and one officers were retired from the active Navy list of officers, without trial or notice, or record of any sort, was not in accordance with the principles which our Government recognizes as the only guarantees of judicial fairness and impartiality.

2. *Resolved*, That the General Assembly does not assume to criticise the conduct of those who were charged with the execution of the provisions of the law in question, nor to express an opinion as to the propriety of the removal of the officers retired under the action of the board; but it intends to affirm the principle that every officer of the Army and Navy of the United States has the inalienable right to be heard in his own defense, and to confront his accusers, when charges affecting his personal character and professional honor are brought against him.

3. *Resolved*, That for reasons hereinbefore alluded to, the Senators and Representatives of Virginia in Congress be earnestly requested to coöperate in effecting the passage of a bill which shall provide a fair opportunity to the parties aggrieved by the action of said board, to vindicate their tarnished honor; and subject not only them, but the whole Navy, to a proper reform, upon just, rational, and legal principles. The form of this remedy it refers with confidence to the discretion of the Representatives of Virginia.

4. *Resolved*, at the same time, That this General Assembly owes it to the rights and the honor of its constituents, involved so largely by the action of the aforesaid board, to declare that it finds on the list of dismissed Virginians, names of men who have, by their achievements in war and peace, in arms and in science, not only commanded the thanks and the compliments of their own country, but had extorted, and, whilst this board was in session, were extorting the homage and admiration of all the great commercial and naval Powers of the world.

5. *Resolved*, That the clerks of the two Houses be directed forthwith to forward copies of these resolutions to our Senators and Representatives in Congress.

Adopted March 5, 1856.

Teste: SHELTON C. DAVIS,
Clerk of the Senate.
S. G. TUCKER,
Clerk of the House of Delegates.

Mr. HOUSTON. Mr. President, I rejoice that the Old Dominion has spoken on this occasion. Her weight in the Confederacy, the peculiar position which she has heretofore occupied, and which she still occupies; her sound political adherence to correct principles in times past, with as few aberrations from a proper course as it was possible during the period of her existence for any State to pursue, entitles her to an attentive hearing. I am informed that California, too, the youngest sister of the Confederacy, has spoken on this subject, though officially her voice has not yet been heard in this Chamber.

Allusion was made the other day by the honorable Senator from Delaware, [Mr. CLAYTON,] to the influence exerted around these walls, and the appeals made to members of Congress by persons who think themselves aggrieved by the action of the naval board, as though members felt it necessary that they should have prompters to stimulate them to the discharge of their duties, and as though they had not innate principle enough to discern right from wrong, and to pursue the right in preference to tolerating the wrong. I wish it distinctly understood, as the allusion was directed particularly to myself, that no outward influence has operated on me to direct me towards the course which I have taken, and which I am determined, with my humble abilities, to maintain upon this floor, and before this nation, in vindicating men who have been relentlessly stricken down, regardless of their rights as officers and as citizens of the United States.

Sir, I will refer to some remarks of mine on a

former occasion—not for the purpose of sustaining myself in the assurance which I have given, but for explanation, and to show the reason why my mind, as early as November 23d last, had arrived at the conclusion which it now maintains. On an occasion when it was fit that I should address my fellow-citizens in reference to the subject now before the Senate,—alluding to the Administration and its component parts, and particularly to the Secretary of the Navy, [Mr. Dobbin,]—I said:

"In the administration of the affairs of his office, I believe he gives general satisfaction; but if I were to rely on the intelligence of the day, as derived from the newspapers, I am inclined to think that, in the action of the naval board, most flagrant injustice has been done to many officers of the Navy; and if impartiality has not been carried to an improper extent, injustice has certainly been done to many of the officers. But as this will be a subject of examination, I will merely make this hypothetical remark."

Sir, this shows that I needed no prompting, after my arrival in Washington city, and that no influences were exerted upon me; but that it was the prompting of my own heart, from a knowledge of the individuals who had been stricken down, which guided my action.

It will not be considered egotistical when I refer to days past, as they form a portion of the history of the country, and when the reference is not made for the purpose of complimenting myself; but it is to me a subject of gratulation and delight, that I had an instrumentality in placing in his proud position in the service one of the distinguished officers of the Navy. In 1825, when a Representative from the State of Tennessee, I obtained a midshipman's warrant for Matthew F. Maury, who then entered the Navy. I have watched his career since with paternal solicitude. I have gloried in his prosperity; and his distinctions I have always considered as reflecting honor upon myself, while the nation was honored by his achievements; and though they were not on the quarter-deck where scuppers run blood, he has built his name high in the niche of fame. It will not be obscured by the action of this mysterious board, who have reviewed his conduct. They may strike him off, and embarrass his prospects as an officer of the Navy, if they please, should their action be indorsed; but they cannot limit the world-wide fame which he has acquired, nor can they snatch from him that wreath of civic glory that his own exertions have won, and which is equal to the laurels he would have won if he had been called to the field, unless he had been altogether unlike the Maurys of the State in which he was reared and his kindred blood, for it was the best of the Huguenots. Sir, it has been stated by the honorable chairman of the Committee on Naval Affairs, [Mr. MALLORY,] that he looks upon Lieutenant Maury as a civilian, and he thinks that great favors have been done to him. He says that Maury has often been withdrawn at his own instance from sea-service; and that he had asked for his present position at the Observatory; but the latter statement was afterwards corrected by the honorable chairman, and very justly. He did not petition for a situation at the Observatory. It was not in time of war that he asked for release or respite from duty. It was not when the enemy were in hostile array on our borders, nor when we were invading a foreign country with our squadrons, that Maury ever asked to be recalled from service.

But, sir, Maury has been taunted by a lieutenant on the board with his civic distinction, his ease, and quiet; while the same lieutenant thinks that it is hazardous, and troublesome, and disagreeable to perform the seafaring part of an officer's duty. I have noticed these taunts. I do not know the individuals from whom they emanate, but they excite in me no indignation. I considered them beneath the contempt of a statesman. I have acquaintance with but one officer of this board, and I should not know the others if I saw them. I shall never seek their acquaintance until the stigma they have placed on themselves by the course they have pursued is taken from their names and characters.

It appears that Lieutenant Maury has been long employed on shore duty. I find, on a comparison of his term of service with that of the chairman of the board, Lieutenant Maury was but four per centum below him in sea service, notwithstanding the great benefits he has rendered to mariners and the commerce of the world while on shore duty. The chairman of that board (Commodore Shubrick) has been in the naval service forty-nine years, of which seventeen years and ten months have been employed in actual sea duty. Lieutenant Maury has been in the service thirty-three years, of which more than nine years have been employed at sea, notwithstanding the misfortune of having been crippled, from which he has entirely recovered. To say that he was not an efficient officer ashore and afloat is not sustained by facts. Lieutenant Maury has not shrunk from the responsibilities of a commander at sea, for during the Mexican war he made application for service in his proper rank, and it was declined. Deficiency cannot be charged to him. As for his sea service, it is thirty-three and one third per cent.; while Commodore Shubrick's is but thirty-seven per cent. of his whole length of service. That, therefore, cannot be the cause for disrating him. It was not the inefficiency of individuals that caused them to be stricken down. No, sir; it was a system of espionage on the Navy; it was a combination; and, as characterized by a distinguished member of the navy board, it was a "packed conspiracy" to strike down chivalrous and gallant men, and give position and promotion to those who grasped the scepter in their hands and wielded it with despotic sway.

You may say it was the fault of Congress. I admit it was a great error to pass such a law as the one under which this action has taken place; and if its passage was commended to us by any who understood what would be the result, it was a culpable act—it was a criminal act. I have no doubt I voted for it, though I have not referred to the record; but if I did vote for it I voted without comprehending it. I deferred to the committee and the Department, supposing everything was for the best. I was not importuned to vote against it, and I supposed it must all be right. I imagined that some two or three dozen officers would be withdrawn from the service who were inefficient through age or wounds or infirmity, or from habits intolerable in the Army or the Navy, and which reflected no credit on the service. Never did I dream that those dropped would amount to fifty. If I commited the sin of voting for the bill, it was the sin of ignorance amounting to omission only; though I may be properly censurable for not having examined it when it was to fall so weightily on men who deserved their country's thanks for preserving their country's honor. Yes, sir, it was a great offense; and greatly must we atone for it when we reflect on the injustice done to those injured by its operation.

But, sir, has the law been carried out impartially, fairly, and justly? Who were the persons who went into the board? My honorable friend from Delaware, [Mr. Clayton,] says that one of the distinguished men on it was Commander, now Captain, Du Pont, in whose behalf he presented, (as he always does) a most eloquent, pathetic, and I may say elaborate vindication, the other day, in secret session. He asked that the injunction of secrecy should be removed to allow the publication of his remarks. It was done, and the officer has the full benefit of his vindication. I am glad that his general character is put in issue by the course pursued by the honorable Senator from Delaware. I am willing to take issue on the fact that he is no better than he should be as an officer, and that he is not superior to hundreds who have been stricken down, either in point of seamanship, or in any other high quality which should animate an American naval officer. The Senator says that service on this board was to Captain Du Pont a bitter cup, but the chalice was put to his lips. Sir, he could have declined it. There was no urgent reason why he should not do so. He was a member of the light-house board, and I think he could have declined this service on that ground.

I go further: I intend to show that Du Pont was one of the prompters to this measure; and that, if there has been a "packed conspiracy," he has played a conspicuous part in it. I will not say that he is the Catiline of it, but he played a criminal part. I am not going to take unauthentic newspaper intelligence to prove it, but I will take the Intelligencer—a paper that I venerate for its respectability; and, although I have always been politically opposed to its editors, I have found them gentlemen of veracity. It is entitled to a respect that few journals are now worthy of. Therefore I rely on it. I think it is a document that will cast some light on this subject. By way of showing that it is not a spurious article, and subject to such an objection, I will say, that the article which I propose to read was presented by Mr. Du Pont, and also (as I am inclined to think, though I cannot positively state it) Mr. Magruder, now a flag captain—or some rank whose technical phrase I do not exactly understand—in the Mediterranean. These two officers handed in this publication some time in advance of the meeting of the board. There are other facts which I will bring to bear on this matter, and I will show that the Navy was converted to the use of these men. They may say it was the law that was executed; that the pound of flesh was exacted; that this action was indorsed by the Secretary of the Navy and confirmed by the President; but all this can give no character to the proceeding, if there was corruption or conspiracy in the beginning. If that be the nature of its origin, all the subsequent acts are void. I will not read the whole of this two-column article, but I will read those parts which I think important. What does it say? Listen:

"The scheme submitted by the present able Secretary of the Navy reconciled the apparently incompatible requirements of avoiding ingratitude and a pension, while substituting efficient for incapable men in the performance of active and responsible duties. The plan involved the necessity of the consent of officers of the Navy, for the public good, to accept and discharge the duties with less than the regular compensation of the higher rank; and their patriotism has given a prompt response. Congress have met them in a spirit of equal liberality, accepted their plan for the relief of the service and the country, and placed in their own hands the execution of the law to promote the efficiency of the Navy."

In the hands of the Navy! The Navy comes forward generously and makes this proposition of sacrifice, and Congress accords to them all that their liberality can demand! That is the statement. But again:

"The eyes of the country are on the proceedings of the board with anxious, but confident, hope."

Who cared about it? The country was never aroused to it. The country cared nothing about it, because they knew that our Navy, whenever it came in contact with an enemy, always acted gloriously, and achieved honor for the country, and they were willing to confide it to the proper hands. The people, far off, remote in the interior, had no distrust in our continuous achievements of glory whenever our tars came in contact with an enemy. The country demanded no such thing. It was the Committee on Naval Affairs of the Senate who demanded it. The Senate acquiesced in it, and the House of Representative approved it. It was done without consideration—without the people ever thinking anything about it, and knowing less; yet this assumption is made in this article with great gravity. It continues:

"If it fail in its duty, whether from want of nerve, or want of judgment, or want of honesty, the next Congress will respond to the national demand for an efficient Navy by some short, sharp, and salutary remedy. If officers now sacrifice the country to their interests, they may rest assured the country will have small hesitation in sacrificing them to the paramount necessities of the public service."

I pray, sir, that this may be done. It is all I ask that they may be recompensed "according to the deeds done in their body;" that body means the naval retiring board. [Laughter.] Again:

"This duty, if not thoroughly performed, had as well not be attempted; and the liberal provisions for those found incapable, without their own default, disarms the measure of even the least appearance of harshness, and *leaves no excuse for leniency.*"

We see they were afraid there would be leniency, and this article was to prepare the public mind, and it foreshadows the action of the board. One of the most conspicuous members of the board, and one who contributed more to the passage of the bill through this body than any individual, is the man who foreshadows their purpose in this communication of two columns.

What is the meaning of all this? They cannot rely on age, infirmity, and similar causes, to get old men out of the way and give promotion to aspiring young gentlemen, lieutenants and others; and if these young aspirants cannot get to be commodores, they have made one brilliant step towards it—I mean the brilliancy of two epaulets instead of one. In old times, when we used to do fighting as subalterns, I was very proud when I got one epaulet of silver, instead of gold, and I thought it was the finest thing in the world; but now you can hardly find a passed "middy" who does not want a commodore's epaulets on his shoulders. He likes to strut about to the admiration of the ladies, with his buttons bright and his uniform attractive, and he is a commodore really to all appearances, and beautiful to admiration. [Laughter.]

Mr. BAYARD. Will the Senator state the date of that article?

Mr. HOUSTON. May 21, 1855; and I would ask the Senator to attend to it, for I know he can criticise it with more ability than I can command. Again, the article says:

"This duty is confined to the naval board. With them rests the responsibility of executing or failing to execute the law. They reap many of the advantages, but the country has the greatest stake in the result; and the country will hold the board responsible for the attainment of the results they anticipated when vesting these ample powers of purgation in the officers of the Navy itself."

Yes, sir, they reap advantages from it. They have not merely promoted themselves, but they have promoted their kindred in subordinate ranks. That is generous—is it not? Sir, a system of nepotism has grown up in the country that must be stricken down; it shall not confront the majesty of a free people, and will not be countenanced and fostered by my vote on any occasion while I live; but it has been done by this board. A majority of the captains were family relatives. I am not going into the privacy of families, but this is a public matter, and I have a right to refer to it. Not only were the captains related to each other, but most of them had relatives, subordinate to them, either midshipmen or lieutenants, who were promoted by the operations of the board. Were they impartial judges? Were they competent, honestly, to adjudicate the rights of noble men, who had fought for their country, who had gallantly bled for it, and who had borne aloft its proud banner to the breeze floating over British hulls? Is that to be countenanced? Could no other disinterested men in the Navy have been obtained? Surely, no one will make such a statement.

Do not understand me as casting blame on the Secretary of the Navy. He is a very polite and elegant gentleman, and perhaps he did not inquire into these things. I blame these men for not each telling him, "Sir, my situation is too delicate. If I should find it necessary to remove one above me, it would leave me liable to the imputation of making a vacancy to give place to myself and get promotion. If I remove one who is subordinate to me, and advance my relatives, nepotism will be imputed to me. My honor would be impeached by serving on this board, and I will vindicate it by a just and generous course—just to myself, generous to my fellowmen, generous to men of chivalry, whom I esteem, and who deserve my esteem."

It is suggested to me that the morning hour has expired; but still I ask leave to proceed with my remarks.

Mr. IVERSON. With the permission of the Senator I will move to postpone the special order to allow the Senator to proceed with his speech. Although it is not the "first speech" of the gentleman, it is his first during the present session. He has been exceedingly modest, and I therefore move to postpone the special order.

The motion was agreed to.

Mr. HOUSTON. Mr. President, I will read another extract from this delectable publication. It says:

"What, then, does Congress charge the board with the duty of performing? The law assumes what the country knows to be the fact, that there are many officers in the Navy in the grades mentioned, incompetent to the prompt and efficient discharge of all their duties ashore and afloat. The law has charged the board to examine into the efficiency of the officers of the Navy, and to report those who in *their* judgment, are so incapable of performing all their duty."

Surely it was their duty to recommend the retirement of those who were incapable of performing sea duty, but there must be evidence of that incapacity. It was not to be presumed from a mere suspicion in the mind of any member or members of the board. There were tests by which inefficiency could be determined; and I will show you that the action of the board, if it be regarded as a judgment of inefficiency, is in direct conflict with the action of the Secretary of the Navy. They have not deferred to him. At the time this "review" took place—at the time when naval efficiency was determined by the naval board, what was the condition of the officers of the Navy? No less than fifty-seven officers who were afloat or on duty at that very time were stricken down by retirement or dropping. Fifty-seven of those then engaged on duty the board said were inefficient, and not capable of performing their duties ashore and afloat.

What was the conclusion of the Secretary of the Navy? He had detailed these men to discharge duty, to the number of fifty-seven, and they were actually performing duties ashore or afloat at the time when they were stricken down by the naval board, which thereby stultified the action of the Secretary of the Navy. One or the other erred in judgment as to the efficiency of these officers. These are the two horns of the dilemma. Gentlemen may swing on either—I care not which; neither is pleasant. You need not tell me that the Secretary of the Navy would detail for sea duty incompetent persons, when there are always hundreds of applicants for active service whom he cannot gratify. Can any candid man believe there was any deficiency in any of those men who were detailed by the Secretary for sea or for shore duty? To suppose so is to impugn the action of the Secretary, and to charge him with incapacity, or a want of integrity to his country. I do not care which position gentlemen assume; one or the other is the case if the action of this board can be sustained, which I do not believe. I do not think that Mr. Dobbin would have detailed an incompetent person for sea duty. I am not prepared to indorse his charitable notions of the board, and his laudatory comments of them, as being the soul of honor; but I perceive that their action is contradictory to his own. But, sir, the same article says further:

"It is the duty of the President to keep the public force on shore and at sea in an efficient state, ready for every emergency. If men are incompetent, no matter from what cause, it is his duty to know it, to ascertain it, and to remove them either by his executive power or by legal proceedings."

So these powers inured to the President and Secretary before, and hence the absolute inutility of the law. There was no requirement for it except to suit the demands of a cabal here in the bureaus. They are nests of iniquity, and they are multiplying; but I want the eggs broken. Again:

"But, whatever be the means adopted, he is responsible for the efficiency of his instruments. Congress have aided his judgment by giving him the benefit of the inquest by the board. They are as free to inquire as the President. They are subject to no other restrictions."

What a pity it is that more restrictions were not placed on them, and then there would have been less ground of complaint to-day. This writer says:

"They pass their judgment subject to the same responsibilities, and they are subject to none other."

How proud, how omnipotent, how far above all revisionary power, how irresponsible they are! Further:

"They are bound to inquire fairly, earnestly, courageously; to be guided by public considerations alone; to give the country the full benefit of their knowledge and experience; to report *the truth* as it shall appear to them;—

They italicize "truth;" otherwise, I suppose, it would have no weight.

—"and to remember, that the blood and dishonor of any disaster to the American arms following from any neglect to report every case of incompetency coming within their knowledge will rest on them, and on their memory. Beyond this, they have no duty, no right, and no responsibility."

Again they go on to say:

"In the eye of the country, the first thing is that American seamen and officers shall not be sacrificed by incompetent commanders."

I shall have something to say in illustration of this position. It is a very good one. See how they enlarge upon it:

"To this everything is subordinate, and for this the board was created. How individuals may be affected—whether the country have treated heroes ungratefully or not—is none of their business. They are charged to see that lives of American seamen, and the higher life of American honor, be neither thrown away nor jeoparded by hands of whose competency they are not convinced. If Decatur were alive, but blind, or a paralytic, or deaf and dumb, or so feeble as to be unable to encounter the hardships of a cruise, it would be their duty to say so, and leave the country to take care of the hero while supplying his place."

Yes, sir; but if he was neither of these, and they were to say he was dumb and blind and old, the statement would be false. Sir, a hundred officers walk about these streets repelling the charge of incompetency. They are practical contradictions to it. Here we are told the duty of the board was to retire an officer when he was incompetent. It is only for that cause, or for misconduct of a flagrant character, that he can be retired, furloughed, or dropped. Every one that is dropped feels that imputation on him. Let me give an instance. The other day my friend from Delaware stated that Captain Du Pont had written letters to Lieutenant Rhind and others for the purpose of getting a contradiction to rumors against Mr. Bartlett, of the Navy, one of the most intelligent, prompt, and sailor-looking fellows I ever saw—a gentleman who was selected by the Secretary of the Treasury to go to France, and was there for more than two years, for the purpose of obtaining improved lights and light-house apparatus. He came home bearing a highly laudatory letter from our Minister, Mr. Mason, recommending him to the special consideration of the Secretary of the Treasury. He was again at sea performing his duty when he was stricken down and degraded, as unworthy of a place in the Navy. Not retired, not furloughed, but dropped entirely. That is Mr. Bartlett, to whom my friend alluded the other day, and whose character Captain Du Pont was so anxious to vindicate that he wrote a letter about him; but the answer came too late, and he was dropped for other reasons, it is said.

On a charge being made against him, by rumor, ten years ago, Lieutenant Bartlett demanded an investigation by court-martial or court of inquiry against his accusers. His demands were made to his superiors, and are there yet. He has from time to time demanded an investigation, a court of inquiry, or a court-martial, and it was not given him. Why? They who made the charges knew they could not prove them. The fact that he was continued on service shows that the rumors had no influence on the Secretary of the Navy or his commanders; and yet that man was dropped from the list of officers. Mr. Du Pont had written to different individuals to know if they knew anything about a certain transaction; but the answer, it is said, came too late! Bartlett is a fine officer; but he has one outrageous fault in the eyes of some gentlemen. He is similarly situated with Captain Levy, of the Navy. He was the first man who discountenanced flogging in the Navy; and he has finally triumphed. Bartlett was a temperance man, and recommended dispensing with grog in the Navy. This was offense enough to some gentlemen to incur reprobation, and to brand him as a victim necessary for the sacrifice. Yes, sir, that is it. If Mr. Du Pont had such great solicitude and anxiety for Mr. Bartlett, is it not strange, as a member of the board, having the Secretary's ear, that he did not prevail on the Secretary to give Bartlett a trial, and let him vindicate his character? He requested it promptly. Why not give him a court of inquiry or a court-martial to enable him to exonerate himself? Mr. Du Pont had sufficient influence with the Secretary, undoubtedly, if the Secretary needed a prompter and was disposed to serve him. But no, his feelings of friendship were all dormant until they were awakened by the responsibility devolved on him as a member of the naval board! But, sir, I desire to continue the reading of the article of which I have already given some extracts:

"Of course clamor will follow the report of the board if it be searching and efficient; but worse clamor will follow those who fail to report searchingly and efficiently; for this act is no sudden freak of Congress;"—

If it is no sudden freak, I should like to know when was it deliberately considered.

—"it is the preferred among multitudes of rejected predecessors; it united many conveniences and avoided many objections; it was fully debated, thoroughly considered, and scanned by hostile interests." * * * * * "But the American people are both practical and liberal, and therefore, while providing for removing 'dry-rot,' and substituting sound material, they took good care of the relics and memorials of former glories and long services rendered the Republic. They justly discriminate. It is only those whose incompetency is the result, not of time, nor natural decay, nor hard service, but of their own fault or excess, who 'are to be stricken altogether from the rolls.'"

Lieutenant Bartlett was dropped at a time when the Secretary had detailed him for active duty. He was an accomplished and an efficient officer on ship. Now, remember, it was only for inefficiency that they had any right to touch him. The officers of the Navy were amenable to the laws of the country, and to the prerogative of the Executive, if they failed in their duty; but the board had no power to touch a man for any offense unless incompetency, either of mind or body, unless the *inefficiency* of the gentleman was such that it was impossible to retain him.

This is admitted by these very gentlemen themselves. They say:

"It is only those whose incompetency is the result, not of time, nor natural decay, nor hard service, but of their own fault or excess, who 'are to be stricken altogether from the rolls;' a provision in the law inserted and insisted upon by the people's immediate representatives."

The people, as I have before remarked, knew nothing about it—cared nothing about it. The members of Congress were in the same position in which the people were, and represented them very faithfully—neither the people nor their representatives thought anything about the consequences. This article abounds in points. There is a richness, a marrow in it, that is worth looking at. Let me read another extract:

"If it be no injustice to remove an officer who cannot discharge his duties, it is surely not illiberal to give him the full leave-pay of his rank, when doing nothing; and, if his sensitive honor shrink from receiving pay without rendering service, the law satisfies even this scruple of a high nature, by reserving the liability to duty at the call of the President; and the emergencies of active warfare may well occasion many a demand for experience and skill in dock-yards and shore-batteries, fitting out flotillas, and organizing men for victory, which will satisfy the longing for active service which the note of war will awaken in the oldest naval heart."

It appears, then, that the men who are not fit for active service, according to the board's view, are in time of war to be relied on for their experience, and for that purpose are subject to be recalled by the President to active duty, but inhibited from promotion. That is their notion of honor and justice, and the pride of a military man who loves his rank better than he does his life; for it is for position, and the consciousness of it, that he will fling away his life and trust it to the enemy a thousand times. Yet you tell him by your law that he cannot have that rank and promotion, but he may be recalled to service on the retired list. He may go and fight a battle; he may gloriously defend a post; he may give his life if he chooses; but it must be with the consciousness in his dying moments that, if he had survived this glorious achievement, and if it had been possible to avoid this sacrifice of life, the road of promotion would be blocked—eternally blocked from him. Who will fight your battles under such circumstances? No brave nor honorable man. Such a suggestion as this seems to me to be unseemly; but I suppose it must be imputed to ignorance of human nature and of the foundations of true chivalry. What is the intimation? That these old retired veterans, condemned by the board as unfit for active service, could be useful in organizing for victory during active warfare; and for this purpose to be liable to be called into active service in such a contingency. What a commentary on the whole proceeding!

I come now to the charitable part of this article:

"The investigation should necessarily be secret. It must be so in order that it may be efficient and free. It could not be open without exposing to inquiry, characters whose fitness was questioned, but approved. Doubtful cases must exist; facts casting suspicion which would not be fit to act on, but which would cast a shadow on the public mind, will be elicited. Even those reported against may well be content to ascribe their removal to the vague ground of disability, rather than have their deficiencies specified and paraded before the public."

Ah! there are many things which these gentlemen, I presume, would not wish to have exhibited and paraded before the public; hence they feel the benefit of secrecy and appreciate its value to themselves. From this appreciation of their own conduct, their deductions are drawn in relation to others who are honorable men, willing to confront any imputation which they may dare to bring against them before the public, or before the constitutional tribunals of the service. Where a man has been dropped for alleged infamous conduct, without a trial, they say he might be afraid to have the reasons why it is done paraded before the public! This assertion is made as to every man whom they have damned with a brand of infamy as set forth in the statute, for it is only for infamous conduct that a man was to be removed. They have placed that brand on him, and then say that he might not wish to have it talked about!

Again: "It is in the nature of an executive proceeding." How learned this board were. My friend from Delaware said that a book was written by Mr. Du Pont, and I suppose, therefore, that he is learned. He appears to have been a man of learning, at least in this matter, for he says:

"It is in the nature of an executive proceeding. The President scrutinizes in secret the officer he appoints or refuses, and the Senate closes its doors when considering the fitness of executive nominations and scrutinizing individual character."

Now, I desire to call attention to what Mr. Du Pont and his coadjutor says in this article of the officers of the board, of whom he was one, and his coadjutor another. There must have been something very self-felicitating in the feelings of these gentlemen when they wrote this article, or had it written, because there are various rumors about it:

"The characters and responsibilities of the officers are a guarantee of the faithful performance of their duty, and publicity would only create a combined effort among those impeached to protect each other by destroying the work of the board.

"One observation remains: Congress has allowed captains alone to pass on captains. The other members of the board will be present and witness their proceedings, but without power to affect the result. The indifference, not to say hostility, which has been exhibited generally by this grade of officers to this great measure of reform has, it cannot be denied, created some misgivings, in and out of the Navy, as to the course which might be pursued by the representatives of this grade on the board; but these misgivings have doubtless arisen from the peculiar organization of the board, the law vesting such paramount power in five of the fifteen members composing it, than from any doubt in the high integrity and sense of duty of the captains likely to be selected. We will not entertain the *shadow* of a doubt, that they will execute the stern but imperative duty required by Congress in a manner altogether consistent with the highest honor known to the naval profession. Should it be otherwise, the whole proceeding will be a failure; *but fortunately the reason of the failure will be as apparent as the fact, and Congress will know how to apply the remedy; and should it find that any grade has no stomach for exercising discipline over its fellows, Congress might think it worth while to try the sharper appetite of their juniors, whose interests will coincide with their duty.*"

Oh, a monstrous thing it is if men combine to obtain redress for wrongs which have been done to them! It is looked upon as a heinous offense, if men who have been stricken down and assailed, and who have had their honor wounded, repel the attack with becoming manliness. This is looked upon as a conspiracy, though it is simply the redress of wrongs perpetrated by packed conspirators. It is thus characterized by a distinguished member of the board. They were afraid lest the work of the board should be destroyed, and they thought it was very desirable that it should remain, because by it they were all benefited—greatly promoted. All, or nearly all the principal men on the board had relatives who were benefited by it. It would be a pity to spoil a work so agreeable and family-like in its nature—a very great pity! But, sir, let me give you another extract:

"Congress has, however, confided to the high sense of, duty of the officers of the Navy the interests of the country.'

Beautifully have they requited that confidence—have they not?

"Congress has provided active service and higher rank for the young and aspiring; ease, honorable retirement, and undiminished pay for the faithful and worthy who have become worn out in the public service; and, in order that this may be done without any additional call upon the public Treasury, the younger officers of the Navy are ready to perform the more responsible duties of higher rank without demanding the full pay of the rank. And the country looks to the Navy to *reform itself*—but *reformed it must be!*"

This statement is made by Mr. Du Pont, for he handed in the paper for publication; and it is his—that act made it his. To him belongs the responsibility; and I hold him responsible to the nation—measurably responsible for the outrage that has been done to the country, for the wrongs to individuals, and for the mutilation of our Navy—the destruction of its efficiency, and the annihilation of its chivalry.

But, sir, it is admitted that there are some "hard cases" resulting from the action of this board. The chairman of the Committee on Naval Affairs has said in his report, that there are some hard cases; but I tell you that some of the hardest cases yet remain in the Navy. [Laughter.] There are cases of manifest wrong and injury to men who have been disrated; but the change has given no increased efficiency to this arm of national defense. I can point to many competent and efficient among those who have been dismissed for alleged inefficiency. I have already referred to Mr. Maury's case, and here I will say that he has never visited me; I have never spoken to him during the present session but on one occasion, when I met him at the President's House, and passingly saluted him. He has not called on me; he has not implored me to vindicate his character, and sustain him as a friend. Nor have other officers done this. I have sought them for information to ascertain, if possible, the wrongs inflicted on them, so that I might, in my plain and humble way, as far as I could, vindicate them, and repel and ignore the charges brought against them; but they have not sought me.

What next? Towards the conclusion of this two-column article, I find this language:

"The naval board is charged to scrutinize the men of the Navy, to name those unfit for every exigency of active service. The President is directed to remove such as are so designated from the actice-service list. If the board fail in its duty, Congress will find a remedy and a mode of executing it. More than one radical measure of reform has been proposed: four-year appointments, vacating all commissions, and the like. The moderation of the people, of the majorities in Congress, and faith in the high-minded honor of naval officers, have prevented such rash courses."

It is a pity that these considerations did not prevent the board from taking so rash a course as that which they have pursued. Confidence in the honor of naval officers would have saved some of the chivalry and *élite* of the Navy. Some of its proudest spirits have been sent adrift. Who are now in their places? Men of superior qualifications, superior merit, superior moral standing, or superior worth? Not at all; but their places are vacated; they have not been properly filled. The article thus concludes:

"But if Congress see that they not only have among them men who are inefficient, but also that the whole body is infected so as to be incapable of applying a remedy, they will find a short cut to the conclusion that there is little of the old material worth preserving. They may relieve themselves of the trouble of picking the sound out of the rotten by cutting off all together."

Sir, rather than submit to the action of this board, by which rank injustice has been perpetrated; rather than submit to the wrong which has been done to generous and manly spirits who have served their country; rather than suffer under the wounded feelings of honorable men, the blighted expectations and hopes of their families, their children dishonored, their wives' happiness destroyed and feelings crushed, I would vote to repeal—*repeal*—REPEAL every act that recognizes a Navy in the country, and would see every vessel scuttled to the bottom of the ocean. We can rebuild ships; we can obtain artisans and materials to replace our vessels; we have resources which could be thus expended, though it would take our surplus revenue. Still, sir, though we may have mints to coin silver and gold, we have no mints here to coin gallant hearts. No, sir; the generous, noble heart is coined in nature's mint, and struck in the die of Divinity. It is there that we are to look for seamen. It is an impress which can never be given by the present organization of the Navy; but degradation and dishonor will be brought upon it. My friend the chairman of the Committee on Naval Affairs has said, that Commodore Stewart's dead body might, upon a ship of war, cause Victory to perch upon her pennant, but that you might fill her with Maurys from keel to deck and it would not cause one thrill in a sailor's heart. Was that remark intended to disparage the just claims of Maury to admiration? His scientific attainments are too great for that; but he has qualities aside from his scientific attainments. He was a sailor who performed his duty—or his comrades belie him—so long as he was at sea; and he was at sea a fair proportion of his time. He was a fine sailor and a fit man; but the nation could not dispense with his services in his present position, or he would have participated in the war with Mexico, and there have shown his gallantry and daring.

Mr. MALLORY. Does my friend wish me to answer the question which he put a few moments ago?

Mr. HOUSTON. Yes, sir; if the Senator pleases.

Mr. MALLORY. The honorable Senator asks whether the remark to which he alludes, made by me on a former occasion, was designed to disparage the claims of Lieutenant Maury. Certainly he could not have listened to all that I said on that occasion, or it would have been unnecessary to ask the question now. I occupied a very considerable portion of my time in extolling those services, by comparing him with the first mathematicians and astronomers that the world has ever known; but those remarks were in consequence of, and followed an attempt, as I understood it, to contrast the services of Lieutenant Maury with those of Admiral Nelson. So far from disparaging Lieutenant Maury's attainments as a philosopher, I expressly conceded that they were of the highest character; but I did say that they did not constitute a title to military command.

Mr. HOUSTON. Then I will ask the honorable chairman what were his deficiencies?

Mr. MALLORY. I am not here to point out the deficiencies of individuals. I have stated the abstract proposition that the highest attainments in science do not constitute title to military command. That is the proposition; and if the honorable Senator will argue it with me, I shall be very happy to meet him. The peculiar deficiencies of any individual member of the Navy, are not before us for discussion; nor do I propose to enter into any personal examinations of the qualifications of any man in the Navy. I know too well the position which I occupy, and the character of this forum, to introduce here a discussion of that character.

Mr. HOUSTON. I am very much gratified at the gentleman's remarks, for they are instructive. He has told us in a few words all that the chairman of the naval retiring board and its members have told us. He has told us nothing of the objections made to Mr. Maury. I have this to say of Mr. Maury: That he has proved himself a sailor, ready for service; and he is one of the first men of his age, and is so recognized throughout the world. If he has distinguished himself in science, and under the orders of the Government of the United States has been detailed for shore duty, it certainly does not disqualify him for active service, because there is not employment for one half, or one third, or one fifth of the officers of the American Navy, I believe, by manning all the vessels which we have. If he is employed on shore, there are others who, for the increased pay, are always anxious to go to sea There are more than can get employment. And while he is profitably occupied for the benefit of the country, and while he is shedding a halo around its name, and rendering it illustrious as far as Christendom extends, I think it a small offense that he is a votary of science; and he should not be stricken down for the reasons intimated by one of the gentlemen of the board.

But what was the situation of the board? They were all indorsed by the Secretary of the Navy as they were detailed for that service; and therefore, of course, all doubts of their merit were put out of the question. Now, sir, there are in this matter some of the most striking and singular coincidences of which it is possible to conceive. It is a singular coincidence that these men should have been detailed, and that most of them should have been associated formerly, and that this detail should have been under the circumstances under which it occurred. The honorable Senator from Delaware says that it was against Captain Du Pont's desire that he served on the board, and I must take it for granted, because he says so. I have no doubt such is the impression on his mind; but, when the facts are investigated, the same conclusion cannot be arrived at by any one who has not a personal acquaintance with Captain Du Pont, and has not received his personal assurance to that effect.

Now, sir, I like to see things work evenly, smoothly, clearly, and fairly; and to show that no charge of delinquency of a public character had ever been made against Lieutenant Maury, I will, in a very short time, advert to the circumstances; but in the mean time I must relate an anecdote connected with this subject. What I shall relate comes from such a source that it cannot be doubted; and I will name the officers for fear that an unjust reflection or a compliment—I will not say which—might be cast on others.

Commanders *Magruder*, *Pendergrast*, *Du Pont*, and others, who (at least the last two named) became members of the board, were, as they often were, in conclave in the office of the "INSPECTOR OF ORDNANCE"—not that the gallant old officer who presided in that office united with them, for *he did not*—as I said, these officers were there, and very busily engaged in conversation; and, on the entrance of the "*Inspector of Ordnance*," they rose and left the room, when he picked up the *Naval Register*, and observed on the margin the names of some *thirty or thirty-two commanders* marked with the letters R., F., D., (*reserved, furloughed, dropped.*) He remarked, "You have been *hard* on your grade;" when *Magruder*, who had remained when the other conspirators left—(having *dotted* their commanders)—took the Register and observed, "*We were merely amusing ourselves by looking over the list;*"—an agreeable *amusement*, certainly! The conference was consequently broken up. They were, as Antony would say, "dotted." But he had counted the *thirty-two* names of the persons who had been proscribed, and this was *weeks before the board met.* Yet, it is said, everything was decided by a vote after the board met in June. The Secretary of the Navy detailed the officers only a few days previous to the meeting of the board—the 5th of June. On the 14th, two of the members arrived at New York, and were immediately summoned from there. These two were Commodore McCauley and Captain Stribling. They were summoned, and they sat on the board. I shall have something to say of them presently.

I wish to do justice to everybody. In order to do justice we must understand the case; and for that purpose I have the information requisite to place the character of one of the members of this board in a situation that will enable the Senate to determine whether the decision of officers, such as he, could be of that impartial, pure, and immaculate character necessary to give it weight and influence, not only with the American Senate, but with the American community.

Mr. MALLORY. Permit me to ask the honorable Senator to repeat the names of the parties of whom he has spoken? I believe he has named some who were not on the board.

Mr. HOUSTON. Mr. Magruder was not on the board, but it was understood that he was the principal arranger. He was there at the time I mention, but he was not on the board.

Mr. MALLORY. What were the names?

Mr. HOUSTON. I cannot speak positively as to names, but I will give them as I understood them. I have no memorandum, and may be incorrect. They were Magruder, Du Pont, Pendergrast, and others.

Mr. MALLORY. Did I understand the honorable Senator to say that there were thirty-five captains marked?

Mr. HOUSTON. "Dotted."

Mr. BAYARD. Do I understand the honorable Senator to state these facts upon the authority of a particular individual, or on rumor?

Mr. HOUSTON. On the authority of Commodore Skinner—that is all.

Mr. BAYARD. Did the honorable Senator say Commodore Skinner told him the names?

Mr. HOUSTON. I am not certain as to the names of all; but there were two or three of them who were afterwards on the board. Now, we must look at a very important matter in relation to Captain Stribling. I call the attention of the honorable chairman of the Committee on Naval Affairs to the circumstances. I believe he says that when a midshipman quits the Naval Academy he is considered qualified to command a frigate.

Mr. MALLORY. Theoretically.

Mr. HOUSTON. But if he cannot do it practically it is of no use; for theory never did anything in the world worth speaking of. Are they qualified to do it practically?

Now, sir, I intend to consider the case of a gentleman who was a member of the board—a distinguished scientific gentleman—who was, as I am informed, four years in charge of the Naval Academy, and was also at one time in charge of the flag-ship of the West India squadron—Commodore McCauley's flag-ship. The gentleman to whom I refer is Captain Stribling. Mark you, he is the gentleman who was to qualify midshipmen to command a frigate when they leave the Naval Academy! We will see how much he knows about the matter, or how little he has done—one or the other. I think it is one of the most pertinent cases I ever knew in my life; and I think some of the acts under it will appear very *impertinent* compared with its pertinency. [Laughter.] I have before me the correspondence in relation to the matter of which I will speak. Captain Stribling was at sea with his ship between seven and nine months. He had been ordered out in the summer of 1854, in the STEAM FRIGATE SAN JACINTO, with a view to proceeding to the Baltic, to protect our interests in the presence of the English and French fleets; but, becoming disabled at sea, put into Boston and was refitted; again refitted twice at Southampton, England; visited France, and Spain, and the West Indies; and returned to Philadelphia in March, 1855, and was immediately ordered to take Commodore McCauley on board, and proceed to the coast of Cuba, to protect our flag from aggression, as the flag-ship of Commodore McCauley in the West India squadron, at a time of great excitement—I think in April last—at a time when it was understood that every American naval vessel which went into the West India seas had authority to strike the enemy whenever they met them, if the slightest indignity was offered to our national flag. In a vessel on such a station as that, everything should have been in preparation, ready at any moment for a conflict with the adversary. If it was not, this gentleman was to blame. He was the captain. He went out in that squadron; and when he returned, an inspection was made of his vessel. I will give you the result of it. Perhaps it is the only vessel ever in the service of the United States that returned in such a condition as that in which this vessel is reported to have been; and the very fact of reporting the truth by a gentleman, who is a very respectable captain and sailor, cost him his epaulets. Yes, he was stricken down; it was a dangerous thing not to be a favorite of that board under the new *régime*. A man was lucky if he came within their favor.

The first letter I will read is the following:

NAVY-YARD, NEW YORK, *June* 21, 1855.

SIR: Under the circular of May, 1849, the United States steamer San Jacinto, Captain C. K. Stribling, commander, recently arrived at this port, has been inspected and examined, and I have the honor to report that the ship was found in a clean and healthy condition.

The crew were exercised at quarters, and the usual evolutions were gone through with. The result of the examination was not so satisfactory as desired, as will more fully appear by the accompanying report from the officers who made it.

I am, sir, very respectfully, your obedient servant,

CHARLES BOARMAN, *Commandant.*

HON. J. C. DOBBIN, *Secretary of the Navy, Washington.*

This is what was written by Captain Boarman, the commandant of the New York navy-yard, to the Secretary of the Navy. It was communicated to the Senate in answer to a call on the Department for the papers.

The officers by whom this inspection was made were W. L. Hudson and H. H. Bell, commanders, and P. Drayton, lieutenant. The report was made on the 19th of June, 1855. Did not the board meet on the 20th? I will proceed to examine this report:

Report of an inspection of the United States steam-frigate San Jacinto, Captain C. K. Stribling commanding, made by Commander W. L. Hudson, senior officer present, this 19th day of June, 1855, at the navy-yard, New York.

Armament.—Two 64-pounder pivot-guns, and eight 8-inch guns of 63 hundred weight, truck-carriages.

1. Date of last inspection: Never inspected.
2. Date of target practice since last inspection: May 10.
3. Time of beating to quarters: 11.39 a. m.
4. Time that the divisions reported ready for action: 11.47, broadside guns; 11.52, bowsprit; 12.10 p. m., stern-pivot.
5. Whether all the divisions were found to be properly prepared: They were not.
6. If any of the preparations are defective, and in what particulars: No wads, no spare shot or shells, were passed up; slings and preventers not up.
7. Whether the men are well trained in the exercise of their guns, and especially in pointing them: They were not well trained.
8. Whether the men are well trained in securing masts and spars in case of loss or injury to shrouds and stays: They were not.
9. Whether the men are well trained in passing powder from the magazine, and thence to the guns: They are.
10. Whether there was any target-firing during the inspection; if there was, make a special report of it: There was none.
11. Whether the men are well trained in small-arms exercise, and in firing: They are not.
12. Whether the boarders, or others, are trained to single-stick or broad-sword exercise: Very few at single-stick, none at broad-sword.
13. The condition of boats, when armed for service: The boats were never fitted for armaments.
14. Whether the boats' crews are expert in the management of the boat and field-guns, and in embarking and debarking, &c. Were not tried for want of arrangements.
15. Time required to shift a carriage on spar-deck: Ten minutes.
16. Time required to shift a breeching: Twenty seconds.
17. Time required to shift a gun from one side to the other for firing: Twelve minutes.
18. Whether the arrangements for boarding and repelling boarders are good, or otherwise: Are not good.
19. Whether the arrangements for extinguishing fires are good: Good, but the hose are short; they do not reach from one end of the ship to the other.
20. The general condition of the vessel, armament, and crew, for efficient service in action: The general condition of vessel and armament is fair; there are, however, some defects that impair her efficiency in action. The powder for shot and shell-guns is passed from the magazine through the same scuttle, and conveyed to the deck by the same elevator; the shell-room floor is too low for dryness; lockers

for solid and hollow shot are situated so that they are passed through the same hatchway, and by the same men.

It is a very serious defect in the arrangement of her battery, there being no bulwarks to protect the guns' crews. In close action, against sharp-shooters, it is believed they could not keep their quarters against the improved arms; and the hammocks being stowed in temporary nettings, over the stern and quarters, are great impediments to clearing the stern pivot for action. On this occasion the time was thirty-one minutes. Wooden bulwarks, with low ports, would answer better, we think.

Thirty-one minutes to bring a gun into action! A steam vessel may go eighteen miles an hour; but suppose she should only run eight miles an hour, one could have run the distance of four miles before this gun was ready to bear on the enemy. They might have sunk or boarded her before it could have been done. Again, they say:

Her crew does not appear to have been sufficiently trained at their guns for efficient service in action.

NOTE.—The ship is in clean and healthy condition, and perhaps some allowance should be made in the above report in consequence of the time and circumstances under which the inspection was made. The commanding officer had been directed to land all the stores, unreave the running rigging, &c., preparatory to the immediate transfer of the crew to Norfolk, most of which was executed when the undersigned received their orders to proceed to the inspection of the ship, as per the above report.

Very respectfully, your obedient servants,

W. L. HUDSON, *Commander.*
H. H. BELL, *Commander.*
P. DRAYTON, *Lieutenant.*

Hon. J. C. DOBBIN, *Secretary of the Navy, Washington.*

Forwarded by CHARLES BOARMAN, *Commandant.*

Then Mr. Dobbin writes to the Captain:

NAVY DEPARTMENT, *June* 22, 1855.

SIR: Inclosed with this you will find a copy of the letter addressed to the Department by the commandant of the New York navy-yard, dated the 21st instant, relating to the examination and inspection of the steam-frigate San Jacinto, together with a copy of the report of inspection.

Very respectfully, your obedient servant,

J. C. DOBBIN.

Captain C. K. STRIBLING, *late in command of the United States steam-frigate San Jacinto, Washington, D. C.*

Mr. Stribling's answer was on the 28th of June—six days after the board met. He was no doubt exceedingly busy, notwithstanding the little advance these gentlemen made in the previous caucus, and the caution which had been given them: he had found himself very much engaged. After six days he found time to answer. Here is what he says:

"WASHINGTON CITY, *June* 28, 1855.

"SIR: I have the honor to acknowledge the receipt of your letter of the 22d instant, inclosing the report of the inspecting officers upon the condition of the San Jacinto. I cannot refrain from expressing my deep regret and mortification that such a report should have been made to the Department.

"In justice to myself and those I have lately had the honor to command, though the responsibility is my own"—

Here is magnanimity—"the responsibility is all my own." That is valorous. I like a man who is willing to assume the responsibility. There is no truckling. He had no dread of arraignment. He felt himself superior to question; therefore the responsibility was his own. The passage continues—

—"I beg leave to call your attention to one or two facts, which, if rightly considered, will, I hope, tend to relieve me from the censure of the inspecting officers, and alter the impression which may have been formed from it, injurious to my professional reputation."

They passed no censure on him; they reported the facts, and no censure is stated, but it is implied in the facts themselves. The facts are a condemnation to the officer:

"It is within the recollection of the Department, that the San Jacinto was exactly two months absent from the United States upon her late cruise. Just before sailing from Philadelphia, more than fifty men were added to the crew, to replace those who had been sent to the hospital, discharged by order of the Secretary of the Navy, and deserted."

And who were they? Was it so difficult to incorporate fifty men with more than three hundred men on board the ship? Some of them were sailors reënlisted; but he wishes to say the fifty had tainted the whole, and ruined the discipline of the whole ship.

"This change of more than one fourth of the *working* men of the crew required an almost entire change of the stations of the men at quarters and other stations."

Now, he had a complete crew without them; and, as he was going into dangerous seas, and carried the commodore on board, it was very important to have the vessel in perfect trim. He had this addition to his force for that reason:

"This change of more than one fourth of the working-men of the crew required an almost entire change of the stations of the men at quarters and other stations; consequently, the drill and exercise of the crew had to be commenced anew. When it is considered that but two months had elapsed from this time until the inspection of the crew and ship at New York, to apply the same rule, or to expect the same expertness, under such circumstances, as would be expected from a crew returning from a three years' cruise, I do not think fair or just. This fact does not appear to have been noticed by the inspecting officers."

It was not their business to notice it.

"In these two months there had been one thorough practice at target with the great guns. As to there not having been any target practice with the small-arms, I did not consider it proper to commence target practice until the men were more thoroughly drilled."

Why, sir, he had about three hundred of them out for nine months previously, in which he might have drilled them; and is not target practice with small-arms a part of the drill of a naval sailor? It is an important part; for, although he may not walk very well, or stand very elegantly, or though he may be a little clumsy with his gun, if he shoots well, that will make up for all his other deficiencies; but he did not want that done. Oh, no! Again:

"The boats were not fitted, as the inspectors state, for mounting and landing the boat-guns; they had, however, been used in the boats, as the reports at the Office of Ordnance and Hydrography will show. The fact that the landing of the stores of the ship had commenced before the inspection, will to a great extent account for any deficiencies at the guns of grummets, wads, shot, &c.; and the dissatisfaction of the crew at the prospect of being transferred to another vessel, under new officers, and all its attendant evils, prevented that alacrity and zeal usually exhibited by a crew about to be discharged.

"I am, sir, very respectfully, your obedient servant,

"C. K. STRIBLING,
"*Captain United States Navy.*

"Hon. J. C. DOBBIN, *Secretary of the Navy, Washington.*"

"All its attendant evils." What are the evils in transferring men to a ship? Only tell them to take up their duds and go—a very important matter! They leave no furniture there, and take none with them but what is personal to them. I suppose these men must have been very unhappy when they came to be transferred to another vessel, because they must have had a glorious, easy, lazy time there, doing nothing, sailing along in a fine vessel, and pretty "clean," too, they say.

Well, now, this explanation is "perfectly satisfactory!" It is nothing but the most flimsy excuse in the world, which would disgrace any officer, for his ship not being in trim in the face of the enemy. If it had been in the military service he would have been shot for such inefficiency, or if spared his life he would have been degraded in rank. This is the first time in my knowledge, or in the history of the Navy of the United States, as far as I am informed, where a vessel was ever reported in such a condition on her return to port. What! the hose too short! Had he not power, when refitted at Boston, or when he came in from his former cruise a month or six weeks before, to call on the Bureau of Construction and Equipment, to tell them of the difficulty, and have everything fitted up—have all the deficiencies fixed, and the vessel in complete order; and if it had not been done then they would have been to blame? He was bound to report to that bureau, and, if he did not, it was manifest to the Secretary of the Navy on this showing that he was deficient and culpable in his duty; and, instead of remaining a member of this board to try his fellow-officers for misconduct, for delinquency, for want of qualification for duty on shore and at sea, would it not have been becoming in the Secretary of the Navy to notify him that he was released from further action on the board, owing to the stigma that had been placed by this report upon his reputation? Was it fit and seemly that he should remain as a judge on gentlemen of chivalry, of carefulness, and attention to their duties? But what did he do? Why he gives him one of the most courteous, kind, amiable responses, perhaps, that has ever been written or printed. The Secretary, after referring in his letter to the correspondence that had taken place, says:

"I deemed it my duty to call your attention to the report, and am gratified that my expectations have been realized in receiving a *satisfactory* explanation."

He called attention to the matter because it was his "duty;" he did not wish to do it! Did you ever see a gentleman so amiable? The explanation was perfectly "satisfactory." He ought to have removed Stribling instantly; and if the President had cognizance of it, and knew his duty as an executive officer, instead of placing him in a position to strike off the heads of honorable men—men who had performed their duty, and discharged the trust which the Government demanded of them, and strictly adhered to discipline and principle—he should have relieved him from further service by notification that, "by virtue of the prerogative placed in my hands by the Constitution, I relieve you, Captain Stribling, from further service—notwithstanding you have been the foster-father"—no! I beg pardon of my distinguished friend from Delaware—I believe it was Captain Du Pont who was the foster-father of the Naval Academy; but this gentleman was the principal there—was at the head of it for a long time.

What will be thought after this exhibition—the strangest that has been made in the face of the American people or the American Senate? This gentleman was at the head of the Naval Academy for four years; and we must look for bright "middies" when they come out from there, after graduating, to take charge of our frigates and men of war. Is it not a beautiful commentary upon their chances? Yes. These are the men who are to build up the Navy, give it efficiency, and remove the "dry-rot." Sir, this is one that I would call a hard case—one of the hardest cases in that line of business in the Navy. [Laughter.] But it is entitled to some distinction because it is without a parallel.

But, sir, my friend from Delaware has said that Captain Du Pont has done a great many things, and, amongst others, that he absolutely wrote a book for which he received great commendation; but, sir, that book has given him no very great credit, according to the fact which I shall proceed to state. Du Pont was a member of a board appointed by Secretary Kennedy in the fall of 1852 to prepare a code of rules and regulations for the government of the Navy, approved and issued in March, 1853, a few days before the change of Administration. The present Secretary, entertaining doubts upon the subject, submitted the case for the opinion of the Attorney General, who pronounced it "null and void," the board having exceeded its jurisdiction. This PRINTED CODE, forming a volume of *two hundred and fifty pages*, and costing *many thousand dollars*, became a dead loss in consequence of *this board* having no definite knowledge of matters more legitimately within their province than framing and executing laws to promote the "efficiency of the Navy."

You see what a latitudinarian this fellow Du Pont is. [Laughter.] There is no telling what he will not have his fingers in; if you give him an inch, he will take an ell.

This printed code cost perhaps $20,000 to publish; it became a dead loss in consequence of the board having no definite knowledge of the matters legitimately within the provisions while they were framing and executing laws to promote it.

Now, sir, that is the book reputation which Du Pont obtained. It is between him and the Attorney General; and to tell you the truth, I am somewhat in the situation of the woman when there was a fight between her husband and the bear. She said "I will stand off; I might get scratched if I interfere; I shall not say a word." [Laughter.]

But, sir, I have a great many other things to which I would direct the attention of the Senate; for as I do not speak often, I want to say a good deal when I do speak. I will now read a copy of a letter from the Navy Department to Commodore Hull, dated December 16, 1839. I will remark that this is a copy taken from the letter received by Commodore Hull, but I find in the printed documents among the information called for by the Senate, that the word "sex" is omitted in page 46; but in the copy that I have, that word is used when referring to the action of Mr. Du Pont, Mr. Pendergrast, Mr. Missroon, and Mr. Godon, all of whom were members of this board.

Mr. MALLORY. If my friend from Texas will allow me, I desire to ask from what that copy is taken? Is it a departmental copy?

Mr. HOUSTON. It is not a departmental copy. I went to the Department, and the copy there contains the error which is in the printed documents on our tables; but the sense will show, as do also the circumstances notorious at that time, that the disrespect to Commodore Hull's family was one ground of complaint between these officers and the commodore. The insertion of the word "sex" will make it sensible, and without that word it will not be so.

Mr. MALLORY. I only ask that it may appear that the copy now read to us is not the copy coming from the Department, which we have printed before us.

Mr. CLAYTON. Will the Senator from Texas allow me one moment?

Mr. HOUSTON. Yes, sir.

Mr. CLAYTON. What the Senator refers to, I believe, is the letter of the Secretary of the Navy, of the 16th of December, 1839. Now, I ask the honorable Senator if he is not perfectly well acquainted with the fact that, after that letter was written, and after Secretary Paulding investigated the whole case, he wrote another letter acknowledging the errors which he had committed, and making ample atonement for the errors in that dispatch of the 16th of December. He acquitted Du Pont and his friends entirely of the accusations made against them. Is not the Senator from Texas perfectly aware of that fact?

Mr. HOUSTON. I will be very happy, Mr. President, to respond to the inquiry of the honorable Senator. If I were disposed to be disingenuous, or to evade the truth in any way, I might do so, but I will not. My friend from Delaware the other day took full latitude in spreading all these disavowals through the channel of the newspapers, so that he is in advance of me; but he did not read this letter; and I will convince him that Secretary Paulding did not, according to his letter published the other day, disclaim what he had before done, or say that it was *ex parte*. I will show what Commodore Hull said in relation to the matter afterwards. I intend to treat the subject with great fairness, and I do not intend to exonerate these men from charges with which they are justly branded, and which neither time nor circumstances can ever wipe out.

Mr. CLAYTON. Does not the gentleman admit that Secretary Paulding says, in his last dispatch, that his dispatch of the 16th of December, 1839, did injustice, and that he virtually retracted the whole of it?

Mr. HOUSTON. Yes, sir: but then he did not say that he was a liar, which he would have to say if he justified them; because he stated facts, which he never revoked. Let the world judge. I will ask that the word may be marked in my speech in brackets to show that "sex" is wanted. My copy is identical with the one taken by Commodore Hull's captain, who was with him on the station when the letter was received. The letter does not make sense without that word. Mr. Paulding says:

"Yet it is with great regret the Department is obliged to state, that no sooner had they set foot on board this noble ship, than the officers of the ward-room, who ought to have set an example of respect and subordination to their juniors, entered into combinations and cabals calculated to defeat every object for which she had been fitted out. They clamored against the arrangements that had been made by the navy commissioners for their accommodation, as if a ship of war were intended for that purpose alone; they lost sight of the respect and consideration due to that [sex] which every gentleman, and most especially every officer, should feel it his pride to cherish on all occasion."

Without the word "sex" it would read:

"They lost sight of the respect and consideration due to that which every gentleman, and most especially every officer, should feel it his pride to cherish on all occasions."

The insertion of that word makes the passage complete, and that it should be there I have no doubt. I shall not insert the word as though it were undoubted; but it shall go to the world that I believe it should be there, and I think my opinion will be vindicated.

Such a charge as that would be a very grave thing, and would impugn the chivalry of the gentlemen implicated; but I will waive all remarks on that, and not attempt to make any capital out of it at all.

The next thing he says is, that Du Pont, Missroon, Godon, and Pendergrast—

—"appealed to the public in communications disrespectful to their superiors, and violated the long-established rules of the service by publishing an official correspondence without the consent of the Department."

I call on my friend from Delaware to notice that, and I ask if Mr. Paulding took that back?

Mr. CLAYTON. Yes, sir, he did.

Mr. HOUSTON. That is a matter of history. Did he take that back, and say that they did not publish an official correspondence without the consent of the Department?

Mr. CLAYTON. He took it all back.

Mr. HOUSTON. No, sir; for that would contradict himself; but he says that he excuses them: and why? Because, after they had been ordered home by Commodore Hull, and had returned, by combination or otherwise, they made most explanatory and satisfactory reports. Yes, sir, the four gentlemen, Messrs. Godon, Pendergrast, Missroon, and Du Pont, made long reports, friends stepped forward no doubt, political influence was exerted, and they were ordered back. Their reputation would have been lost if they had not returned! And when the Secretary ordered them back, he sent a letter to be read on the quarter-deck of the ship, exculpatory of them so far as it could be. He did not contradict those charges which he had made himself, from his own personal knowledge. But think you not that he had personal knowledge of these publications? The charge was such as should have brought dismissal to an officer, and for which his name should have been wiped from the register of the Navy. Certainly we all know that much. I know that such would be the case in the Army, and I presume the discipline of the Navy is equally rigid.

Mr. Paulding never took back that charge, and when he ordered the officers to return, what did they do? They went all over Europe, traveling wherever it was most agreeable. They did not join the ship for five months, and then insulted Hull when they went on board his vessel.

Mr. CLAYTON Will the honorable Senator allow me to ask him what is his authority for saying that Du Pont went traveling all over Europe after being ordered back to the Ohio?

Mr. HOUSTON. His own letter, I think.

Mr. CLAYTON. It is utterly untrue.

Mr. HOUSTON. I have not read all the letters; they are too long and explanatory for me.

Mr. CLAYTON. Then you know nothing about it.

Mr. HOUSTON. Did he not make an apology and explanation?

Mr. CLAYTON. No, sir; he did no such thing.

Mr. HOUSTON. He made no explanation?

Mr. CLAYTON. He did not; I am speaking only of Du Pont.

Mr. HOUSTON. Well, I am glad that he did not. He had no apology, and the others made very bad ones; he is in a worse situation than I thought he was. [Laughter.]

I must now be permitted to say a little about a combination or cabal which existed from the very time they first set foot on that vessel, before she left the port of New York; and they would have been ordered back at once, if it had not been supposed that it was too late to make the necessary transfers in order to supply their places. Captain Smith was the furnishing officer to supply accommodations and other things necessary; and they insulted him in a correspondence which they had with him, or at least Mr. Du Pont did, for I am speaking of him especially.

Mr. BAYARD. It is untrue.

Mr. HOUSTON. I say he insulted Captain Smith.

Mr. BAYARD. In making that statement, will the honorable Senator tell us upon what the allegation rests?

Mr. HOUSTON. On the correspondence.

Mr. BAYARD. In the correspondence, Captain Smith himself says that the letter of Lieutenant Du Pont was perfectly respectful.

Mr. HOUSTON. The Commodore did not.

Mr. BAYARD. I have read the letter, and, if the honorable Senator can make insult of it, he has a power of perversion greater than that which he has already exhibited to the Senate.

Mr. HOUSTON. I do not know how times are now, for it is long since I have been subordinate to rules and regulations; but it struck me, when I read it, that at one time, in 1812, 1813, 1814, or up to 1818, it would have been considered insubordinate to a superior in the Army, and I supposed it would be the same in the Navy. At all events, Commodore Hull, by the return of these gentlemen, felt himself humiliated and degraded. Here is what the Secretary of the Navy said in his letter to these officers:

"Had this combination succeeded in attaining its object, here would have been an end of that power which the laws have confided to the head of the Navy Department, and that respect and subordination so essential to the service; the direction of the Navy would have reverted to those whose province it is to receive and obey orders; and a combination of officers might at all times drive the Department from any measure it thought proper to adopt."

He is speaking of facts within his own knowledge; and this he could not take back when he wrote the exculpatory letter to Commodore Hull, predicated upon their application; and if Mr. Du Pont did not do it I must have overlooked something in the correspondence, for I did not wish to read it all, as it was very voluminous; and, besides, I had a dread of him, for I had read his official report at San José, of which I will speak directly. [Laughter.] It is remarkable in its way.

Now he speaks of Du Pont's letter, and I say he never took this back. Mr. Paulding says:

"The letter of Lieutenant Du Pont is not such a one as I had expected from an officer who had heretofore sustained so high a character in the Navy. It is not couched in language becoming an inferior addressing his commanding officer; and his refusal to accept the concession, of which his brother officers availed themselves, savors more of pettishness than dignity or of manliness."

He took back none of these charges at all; but, to gratify the gentlemen and their friends, he ordered their return. What may we reasonably suppose to have been the cause? The facts had not changed since the first rebuke which he administered; but it would have blasted the young men's reputation if they had been sent home in disgrace by the Commodore. He must save the mortified feelings of them and their friends. It is a natural thing. I believe you will find it in the Navy, to some extent, as well as anywhere else.

But, sir, while speaking of Du Pont's writing, I wish to bring another production of his to the notice of the Senate. We hear of his chivalry, and my friend from Delaware read to us the most remarkable actions I ever heard of. The commodore said it was one of the grandest things that ever was done, and his letter was read, and I intend to have it read again. It is beautifully written, and one would really suppose half Mexico had been slaughtered, and this was a modest recital of the carnage. [Laughter.] It is one of the most extraordinary things I have ever seen. Du Pont landed with one hundred and one men near San José. He marched to Lieutenant Heywood, a mile and a half or two miles across a creek, ankle deep, and he talks of walking across waters, and so forth, making a terrible splurge! Heywood, with thirty men, made a sortie with his little garrison, which he had defended for some weeks, and joined him as he was advancing. He killed a man as he charged, I believe, and wounded several others; and all that was done by Mr. Du Pont was to get four men wounded and two only disabled. He says it was marching in the hottest fire; and when he comes to conclude his official report he says that the number of killed is unknown. [Laughter.] But friendly Californians say it was from thirteen to thirty-five. [Great laughter.] Is not that a large margin? I thought of Falstaff and his buckram men when I read it—two swelling to eleven, I believe, and all Kendall Green coming in to boot. [Laughter.] Lieutenant Heywood corroborates that statement; but they found none of the men who were killed! What complacent boasting! In describing this event, which I have done in two or three sentences, Du Pont occupies no less than four pages of the public documents—the most voluminous communication I ever saw for such an event. Lieutenant Stanley, who, I believe, has been dropped or furloughed—I do not know which—achieved a very handsome exploit, and I think he made his official report to his commanding officer in fourteen lines. He rowed fifteen miles up the beach, landed forty-five men at night, marched twelve miles into the interior, took and spiked three guns—one eighteen feet long, another sixteen and a half, and another twelve and a half feet long. He spiked them—composition guns—and returned safely in the face of an enemy, supposed to number three hundred. He made a little report of fourteen lines; and he is one of the gentlemen who has been overslaughed. Stanley was engaged in three other actions there, and he is one of the most chivalrous and gallant men of the Navy. The only complaint which is made against him is that he is quarrelsome! Sir, I like sailors to quarrel in times of war, and do it effectually. It is a good notion, and I would not discountenance it.

But, sir, from the laudations passed on Du Pont by my friend from Delaware the other day, I do not know but that some other members of the board ought to feel a little irritated and uneasy. He says Du Pont was the leading spirit; that he always leads from the force of his superior intellect. I do not give the language, but I believe I give the general idea. Then he places the rest of the board in a secondary position, although some of them were of superior rank. Really, it is not to be wondered at that this man should be conspicuous here, and should love fame and distinction. My friend did not say that he was not the most modest man in the world. He was not charged with vanity or a love of praise, of course; but a proud and gallant man is, and ought always to be, fond of praise and just laudation. I am furnished with a very remarkable fact in relation to him. I have described the battle of San José, in which that landing took place, the march of two miles, and at the most four wounded. A doctor took out one ball. Really, it was like a fight that took place on the frontiers—I will not say precisely at what spot—but I can prove it by my colleague. It was thought there were about thirteen killed; that was the whole number that could be found; and you know, sir, if a man kills game and does not find it, it is just as good as if it were not killed. They found but thirteen; and when they came to make out the official report it was asked, how many do you think there were? Some one said thirteen. Oh! said another, thirty or forty! Well, said another, there was at least eighty-seven, so put down eighty-seven. [Laughter.] They slept on it that night, and this number did not appear large enough; and the next day an addenda was made to the report, or rather a second report more official than the other, making out one hundred and fifty killed. [Laughter.] It was just so with this account of the Californians; there were between thirteen and thirty-five killed. That is a very wide margin; but there must be something done! The fact is that no one was killed, as far as ascertained, but one whom Lieutenant Heywood killed, charging out with his thirty men to meet Mr. Du Pont, who had one hundred and one men. But he must swell this into importance! Would anybody have thought the marching of two miles, and coöperating with the gallant little band that had been beleaguered there for such a length of time—would he have thought of claiming glory and praise, when Stanley had fought a number of actions, and I do not find that Commodore Shubrick ever thought one of them worthy of a note?

There were others who acted gloriously in the war with Mexico who fared badly. Stevens, the companion of Heywood, who defended that little fort at San José, and who is spoken of in terms the most laudatory and approving, was dropped. Ochiltree—a gallant young fellow spoken of on three occasions in the Pacific—once at San José, another time at Guaymas, and I believe at Mazatlan, was also dropped. The cause of it, perhaps, is that he went on a spree sometimes on land, but never while at sea on duty. That is a terrible thing!

Mr. WELLER. I know him, and he is a man of fine habits, and a gallant officer.

Mr. HOUSTON. He is a gallant, generous, noble fellow; and I know his brother, a citizen of Texas, a man of distinction and ability. Ochiltree bears that reputation. I am glad the honorable Senator from California knows him personally. It is a privilege which I have not; but I would be glad to greet with fellowship a man of his character and nobility of soul. He has been dropped. He is not a drunkard, but I suppose they say he is one of the "hard cases." I have noticed the dropped officers who are in the city. They are gentlemen in bearing. Some I have known for thirty years as chivalrous, elegant men, of fine persons, active, and in the prime of life; yet they have been stricken down, their prospects blasted, and their honor destroyed. These are the men who are unworthy of peership with the gentlemen of the board. They love praise, they love glory too, but they love to earn it before they wear it.

The Senator from Delaware told us that Mr. Du Pont had nothing to dread from an investigation of his character; that he had received the indorsement of the Secretary. It is a singular coincidence that he was associated with Missroon, Godon, and Pendergrast at the time when they were arraigned in 1838, 1839, 1840, and 1841, and when they lay under censure. They have maintained, no doubt, a fine social feeling for each other from that time to this; but is it not a singular coincidence that being indorsed, they should all meet on the board again—all friends again by continuous friendship—united in the ties of brotherhood? Two of them, we are told, have been very unlucky in being called to account for their actions; and my friend thinks the members of the board are not bound to fight everybody of the two hundred and one. I will not encourage reclamation of that kind; but if gentlemen of the Navy happen to cannon on one another and jostle, it is their own business, and they have to settle it. I hold that every gentleman is to be the judge of the injury which he receives, from whom he receives it, and the redress he is to require. I am not going to restrict it. I will discountenance it by a repeal of this law, restoring them all to their proper positions, placing them where they were, and then no wrong can be done. The President will have the power to order a court of inquiry into cases of doubtful utility and character; and upon a court of inquiry reporting the facts to him he has the function to displace such a man from the Navy. Let us create a list for the retired and furloughed; and let him, on the examination of surgeons, determine their disability, and retire them for age, wounds, or disease. By this course we should follow the recommendation of the present Secretary of the Navy. He suggested that he should have the power of recommending culpably inefficient officers to the President for removal; the President should then lay them before the Senate; and the Senate concurring with the President, he should remove every man who was useless, or who did not deserve a place in the Navy. This was suggested by the Secretary of the Navy previous to this unfortunate, and I will say criminal enactment. If this suggestion had been followed, we should have had peace to-day; we should have had the Navy with none in it but those who should be in it; and only those removed from it who were inefficient or unworthy of it. But it is different now. I have not seen or heard of a man who has been removed, who was in the least intemperate, or gave evidence of intemperance; and yet this wholesale charge is made. The officers may, when off duty, for aught I know, indulge; but I say they do not bear that appearance. They are gentlemen, as far as I can judge; and I have sought to become acquainted with them so that I might judge impartially. Unfortunately, I heard of one of the gentlemen who has been retained—but he is one of the "hard cases," I reckon—one of the hardest in the Navy —who was helped into a hotel and carefully laid by to be taken care of: but I do not suppose he meant any harm by it. [Laughter.] It happened just unexpectedly, he not being habituated to it. [Laughter.]

I propose now to gratify the Senate by one of the most tasty and agreeable things I have ever seen. It is an extract from a letter written by Captain S. F. Du Pont, dated "Cyane, off San José, Lower California, March 5, 1848." This is an extract:

"MY DEAR THORBURN: * * * The letter to my soldier friend to replace an official one, was purposely rehanded, that our naval friends, if they felt interested in our doings, might have the benefit."

These are the doings I told you of—nobody killed, nobody hurt.

Mr. BAYARD. What is the date of that letter?

Mr. HOUSTON. March 5, 1848.

Mr. BAYARD. Is it a private or public letter?

Mr. HOUSTON. It is private; but I will give you the name. There is no secret about it; none at all. Listen to the language of this portion of the letter; he thinks he had absolutely electrified the world, and he did not know what would happen. He says:

"But it seems you did not deign to vouchsafe one single word in reference to them."

That is, in reference to the glorious achievements which I have described.

"I candidly confess some disappointment at this, perhaps a little the more as the Cyane had been loud in *trumpeting* the very clever doings at Guaymas of the Southampton, and would have been pleased with even a faint *whistle* in return."

[A shrill and lengthened whistle, such as a boatswain gives when he pipes all hands to quarters, or to grog, was the Senator's illustration of the passage which he read, and it astonished and amused the crowded galleries.]

The Southampton had been lauded and trumpeted, and a little trumpeting here would have been acceptable; but if the trumpeting could not come, they would take the whistle. Well, sir, the letter again says:

"We have been truly gratified yesterday by showers of official and friendly gratulations from Mazatlan, but these certainly would not have made yours less acceptable."

That is on the principle of "you tickle me and I'll tickle you;" but Thorburn did not do this, even after this intimation that a puff might go into the papers, and the poor fellow has been struck down—one of the best sailors in the Navy, I am told, or as good as any. This shows you the love of praise and the laudable ambition of this distinguished man, whose reputation my friend from Delaware [Mr. CLAYTON] thinks is so important to be taken care of. I have not assailed it. I use no epithets. I have used documents. I do not say that a man is dishonest or not a gentleman. I do not say that, whatever may be my private opinion. [Laughter.]

Mr. BAYARD. Will the honorable Senator allow me to see the letter he last referred to?

Mr. HOUSTON. With pleasure, (handing it to him.)

Mr. President, I will ask the Secretary to read a letter from Commodore Shubrick, dated at Mazatlan. I am willing that it shall go into my speech, for I wish to accord all justice to this gentleman. I will use it with more cheerfulness because my friend from Delaware [Mr. CLAYTON] selected it as an evidence of the merit of a member of the board; and for the purpose of sustaining his action and the action of the board, I presume, in the course which they have adopted. I am perfectly willing it should go out to the world in my speech. I wish the Secretary to read the letter.

The Secretary read as follows:

UNITED STATES SHIP INDEPENDENCE,
MAZATLAN, *February* 25, 1848.

SIR: I have the honor to forward herewith reports from Commander S. F. Du Pont, and Lieutenant Charles Heywood, dated 16th and 22d February, and 21st and 22d same month.

I want words to express my sense of the gallant conduct of these officers, and of the officers and men under their command, as detailed in their reports; but feel that I am perfectly safe in saying that the annals of no war can furnish instances of greater coolness, of more indomitable perseverance, of more conspicuous bravery, and of sounder judgment, than are to be found in these details. They will be read with pride and pleasure by the Department, and by every American, and will secure to all concerned a most enviable place in the estimation of their countrymen.

I have the best reason to believe that these reports, so far from overrating the acts of those concerned, are strongly imbued with the modesty of true courage, which adheres to truth, but shrinks from exaggeration, and rather diminishes than magnifies its own deeds.

The satisfaction arising from this brilliant victory over the enemy is clouded by the fall of Passed Midshipman Tenant McLanahan, a young officer of great promise. He received the fatal wound standing by the flag of his country, and died in the hour of victory—an early but enviable death —placing his name high on the roll of those who peril all in the cause of their country, and giving to his afflicted friends the mournful satisfaction arising from the reflection that he has sealed a life of honor with a death of glory.

The presence of the Cyane, and the excellent judgment of Commander Du Pont and Lieutenant Heywood, will, I hope, secure the garrison at San José from further molestation until the measures which Governor Mason informs me he is taking to send reinforcements into the territory can be effected.

I have the honor to be, very respectfully, your obedient servant, WM. BRANFORD SHUBRICK,
Commanding Pacific Squadron.

Hon. JOHN Y. MASON,
Secretary of the Navy, Washington, D. C.

Mr. HOUSTON. This letter says, in one part:

"I have the best reason to believe that these reports, so far from overrating the acts of those concerned, are strongly imbued with the *modesty of true courage.*"

This is evident, because Du Pont, after the trumpet blast given to the gentlemen of the Southampton, was so modest that he was willing to put up with a whistle for the Cyane in return. [Laughter.] It was the modesty characteristic of cool courage, to describe a march of two miles, and killing nobody, as one of the greatest achievements in our annals; and I believe he says, it is "without a parallel." Yes, sir; Commodore Shubrick says, that there cannot be found an instance "of more indomitable perseverance, of more conspicuous bravery, and of sounder judgment." I think the "judgment" in the case was excellent, and I do not wish to detract from it; but he had the cool judgment, either not to go, unfortunately, into danger, or the luck to save all his men and get none of them killed. Therefore, I think that is good judgment, and cool and deliberate courage. [Laughter.] Sir, I have read reports of the battle of New Orleans; I have read of other distinguished battles; I think I have read the reports of the battle of Waterloo; and I believe the first bulletin that come out was not in length equal to this one at San José, and fell far short of it in description. [Laughter.] It may be "modest," but I only want it understood that when you come to sift and analyze it, it is one of the most extraordinary documents ever published; and I do not wonder that a code of laws, or a system compiled by the author of this report, should have been condemned or ignored by the Attorney General, though my friend from Delaware thinks it is very clever. [Laughter.]

My friend from Delaware says that the indorsement of Commodore Shubrick is sufficient for him and sufficient for Du Pont. I have nothing to say in relation to Commodore Shubrick further than as a member of that board, and as a public officer. Not knowing him, it is not my business to cast reflections upon him. I have no desire to do it if I could. In all matters I am disposed to treat individuals fairly; to examine into facts, and from those facts to draw such deductions as I feel warranted in doing. If I am not correct in my deductions, I am aware that the sagacity, and the ability, and the analytical power that is to follow me, will riddle me like hot shot. I propose to examine the records of the Navy, and see whether they are sufficient to induce us to rely upon Commodore Shubrick's indorsement. Lieutenant Maury has been reflected on for having asked to be relieved from service on certain vessels in time of peace. I shall show whether or not that was a justification for striking him down, and whether or not the same rule was applied to the members of the board. I understand, however, that their appointment as members of the board precluded all investigation into their conduct and character. That indorsement ruled out everything like examination or inquiry. Remember, Maury has been reflected on for asking to be relieved from sea service. I wish to read an extract from a letter of Commodore Shubrick, dated the 6th of March, 1837, in which he says:

"On the 2d instant Commodore Biddle arrived. He was kind enough to furnish me with a copy of his order to 'take command of the Pacific squadron' and 'carry into effect the orders of the Department,' and has signified his intention to hold the command during the continuance of the war.

"You will see at once, sir, in how unpleasant a situation I am placed by this *disingenuous*, (respect for the Department alone restrains me from using stronger language,) this *uncandid conduct of the late Secretary*. It cannot be supposed that there is the least occasion for the additional force of the Columbus; and it is clear that, in the opinion of the late Secretary, it was not the Columbus, but Commodore Biddle, that was needed here during the war.

"On making this painful discovery, my first impulse was that I owed it to myself to return to the United States, and I asked permission of Commodore Biddle to take passage in the Savannah. A copy of our correspondence on the subject is annexed, and you will see why I have remained.

"And now, sir, I renew my request to be allowed to return to the United States at as early a day as possible, and in any way that you may please to direct; but I need not say that it would be a gratification to me to return with my pennant on a ship of the size of a frigate at least."

That was Commodore Shubrick on the 6th of March, 1847, in the midst of the war. But what does he say further? I have the correspondence and I will read it, because it is of interest, and because the innuendoes can be as well explained by it as by any language I could use.

UNITED STATES SHIP INDEPENDENCE,
MONTEREY, *March* 5, 1847.

SIR: I have the honor to acknowledge the receipt of your instructions from the Secretary of the Navy of the 16th of May, "to take command of the Pacific squadron," and am sure that the exercise of your command will redound to the honor of the Navy and of the country.

Having been led, by the late Secretary of the Navy, to believe that this command was intended for me, and such appearing now not to have been the case, and being without place in the squadron, I request that you will allow me to return to the United States; taking passage in the Savannah as far as Valparaiso, and thence crossing the Isthmus.

I am respectfully, your obedient servant.

W. BRANFORD SHUBRICK,
Captain United States Navy.

Commodore JAMES BIDDLE,
Commanding Pacific Squadron, Monterey.

Now, I will read the reply of Commodore Biddle:

UNITED STATES SHIP COLUMBUS,
MONTEREY, *March* 6, 1847.

SIR: I have received your letter of the 5th instant. Your return to the United States at this time will be injurious to the service; and will, I think, under the circumstances, be injurious to yourself. The instant information of peace is received—and we may reasonably expect to receive it soon—I shall be happy to transfer the command to you, and leave the station without waiting for instructions to leave.

I wish you would reflect a few days upon this subject, and let me know the result of your reflection.

Very respectfully, your obedient servant,

JAMES BIDDLE.

Commodore W. B. SHUBRICK,
United States Ship Independence.

Let me read Commodore Shubrick's reply to he letter of Commodore Biddle:

UNITED STATES SHIP INDEPENDENCE,
MONTEREY, *March* 6, 1847.

SIR: I have received your letter of this date, in answer to mine of yesterday.

Your opinion, that my "return to the United States at this time will be injurious to the service," is sufficient to decide me, without the few days' reflection that you recommend.

In matters where the interests of the service may come in conflict with my individual feelings, it has always been my rule to yield my own opinions to the opinions of those in whose judgment I have confidence. I do in this case, and will remain in the squadron until I can hear from the Secretary of the Navy.

I am, very respectfully, your obedient servant,

W. BRANFORD SHUBRICK,
Captain United States Navy.

Commodore JAMES BIDDLE,
Commanding Pacific Squadron, Monterey.

In a letter to the Navy Department, Commodore Shubrick says:

"As soon as the Department can turn its attention to the arrangements consequent on a change from the state of war to one of peace"—

This was in 1847, before peace—

—"I hope you will think of my situation, which is as unpleasant as it can possibly be made. I am informed by Commodore Biddle that he has confidential orders to return, and I presume he will leave Monterey soon after I rejoin him. This affords me no satisfaction; what has passed cannot be recalled; and my only wish now is, to return in this ship or the Congress, and leave the command of the Pacific Squadron to some one whose ardor is yet undamped by disappointment, and who will therefore be able to discharge its duties in a manner more satisfactory to the Government."

Here is his last letter:

"To the Hon. JOHN Y. MASON, *Secretary of the Navy, Washington, District of Columbia.*"

—Mr. Bancroft was not then Secretary:

UNITED STATES SHIP INDEPENDENCE,
MONTEREY, *September* 28, 1847.

SIR: Mr. Toler arrived here yesterday in the Preble, from Callao, and brought me several dispatches from the Department, and your letter of the 7th of May, in answer to an application made by me in January last, to be allowed to return to the United States in the Congress frigate, when the terms of service of the crew of that ship should expire.

The arrival of Commodore Jones will be much earlier than I expected, but I have hopes that all that is important to be done on the west coast of Mexico will be effected before his arrival; if not, however, it is my wish to remain, and tender him my services as second in command, so long as he may deem them of importance to the public interest.

I have the honor to be, sir, very respectfully, your obedient servant, W. BRANFORD SHUBRICK, *Commanding Pacific Squadron.*

This was nine days before the Secretary of the Navy gave orders to Commodore Biddle actually to go from the East Indies. This was the 7th of May, and Commodore Biddle was ordered there on the 16th of May.

"In answer to an application made by me in January last, to be allowed to return to the United States"—

This was January, 1847, two months after he got there.

—"in the Congress frigate, when the terms of service of the crew of that ship should expire."

Commodore Jones had then been ordered to relieve Commodore Shubrick.

"But I have hopes that all that is important to be done on the west coast of Mexico, will be effected before his arrival; if not, however, it is my wish to remain, and tender him my services, as second in command, so long as he may deem them of importance to the public interest."

Now, the inference is clearly left to be drawn from this correspondence, that the Secretary of the Navy, Mr. Bancroft, had treated Commodore Shubrick uncandidly, and had concealed from him any intimation of the fact that Commodore Biddle was to be commander on that station. He said that it was disingenuous, and, but for respect for the Department, he would say harder things. When he used such language, the inference is clear that he had been kept in ignorance in relation to it. Was that the case? When he sailed on the 7th of August, 1846, his orders bore this addenda different from the orders which are generally given to commodores:

"Should Commodore Biddle be in the Pacific off the shores of Mexico at the time you arrive there, you will report yourself to him; and, as long as he remains off the coast of Mexico, you will act under his direction in concert with him, communicating to him these instructions."

Mr. PRATT. What is that document?

Mr. HOUSTON. Mr. Bancroft's instruction to Shubrick when he sailed, in August, 1846. Thus it will be seen how the Secretary was chargeable with treating him uncandidly, and to what extent insubordination was carried on by the commodore himself, when he charged the Secretary of the Navy with disingenuousness and a want of candor. He went further, and said there was no occasion for the Columbus in the Pacific. How did he know but that England or some other Power had formed a treaty of alliance with Mexico, and that we should require all the fleet of the United States, and every squadron we had disposable, to defend our coast? We find Commodore Shubrick using his influence to prevent one of the most excellent and efficient vessels in the Navy, the Saratoga, from joining our Pacific squadron. He was willing to take away from the force in the Pacific in time of war not only his own efficiency, if you please, but the means and materiel of meeting the enemy. He knew not what enemies were to be met on that coast; and he certainly ought to have supposed, as a military man and a disciplinarian, that the Secretary of the Navy was the competent judge, and not Commodore Shubrick.

Mr. BUTLER. What ship did the Senator say Commodore Shubrick wished to send home?

Mr. HOUSTON. I said that, by his suggestion, the Saratoga returned from Rio de Janeiro; and in a letter which I have read he says he cannot suppose "there will be the least occasion for the additional force of the Columbus. It is clear that, in the opinion of the late Secretary, it was *not the Columbus, but Commodore Biddle,* that *was needed* here during the war."

Commodore Stockton and Commodore Sloat had preceded him—I believe Commodore Stockton had relieved Commodore Sloat, and Commodore Shubrick Commodore Stockton. Was it not reasonable that he should be relieved from command, if his continuance was not for the good of the service? He was not, in fact, ordered to be relieved; it was a mere intimation. He was not ordered to be relieved by Commodore Biddle until the 16th of May, and he had applied in January previous for leave to return. On the 7th of May, Commodore Jones was detailed to relieve him. Others can judge as well as I can of the propriety of desiring to come home with his pennant when the force in the Pacific was not of a character to give much efficiency to our marine operations. It was weak, even with all the ships we had there, if it was necessary to blockade at a prominent point, and put down resistance to this Government. It is very easy to perceive what is meant, for Commodore Biddle says to him:

"Your return to the United States, at this time, will be injurious to the service, and will, I think, be injurious to *yourself.*"

On reflection, his determination to leave was changed. What the motive was I do not pretend to say; I only state his determination. He had sailed in August, I think, and must have arrived between August and January; and in the month of January he applied for leave to return from the Pacific. He says further:

"This affords me no satisfaction; what has passed cannot be recalled; and my only wish now is, to return in this ship or the Congress, and leave the command of the Pacific squadron to some one whose ardor is yet undamped by disappointment."

What was there to damp his ardor? Was it the fact that he had asked to be returned home in January, and the Secretary of the Navy ordered him to be relieved by Commodore Jones in May, and nine days afterwards Commodore Biddle arrived, sooner than Commodore Shubrick expected? Were these circumstances calculated to damp his ardor or impair his efficiency? No one had complained of his want of efficiency, or of his not having performed his duty to the Government. Mr. Mason had not charged him with delinquency or misconduct in office.

Lieutenant Maury having had his leg broken, when traveling to join a sea-going ship, had to be relieved when his service was not material, and when he was suffering under great bodily injury. If that was a reason justifying his removal, here you perceive that, in time of war, shortly after its commencement, a commodore commanding a squadron asked to be relieved and to be allowed to return home from scenes of active military operations where one of the finest theaters was opened to him—the whole coast of Mexico lay open to his operations, our whale fishermen were out in that sea—and everything opening to him a field of glory. I have not known any occasion during our war with Mexico, except some of the heavy battles, where there was so great an opportunity for reaping glory. I do not say he was wrong in this; but I say that Lieutenant Maury's asking permission in time of peace, when he was suffering bodily inconvenience and infirmity, to be relieved from sea service would not justify the board in striking him down, when Commodore Shubrick, the president of the board, in time of war, when in command of a well-manned and gallant squadron, wished to leave it, after he had been with it only a few months, because his ardor was damped by the disingenuousness or uncandidness of the Secretary of the Navy. The facts show no provocation for the charge of a want of candor, or dissimulation against the Secretary. Sir, if the Secretary of the Navy had instituted proceedings against Commodore Shubrick for using such language, it would have been a matter of grave investigation whether the words were not defamatory, and whether they could be sustained by evidence.

Sir, I have no unkindness of feeling towards the President of the United States or his Secretary of the Navy; yet I do think it very unfortunate, to say the least, that the Navy has fallen within their control and jurisdiction. Neither of these gentlemen, though intelligent and able, had his attention drawn to that department of defense in such a way as to qualify him eminently for its care. Every gentleman who goes into the Navy Department, owing to the condition of the various bureaus there, is placed in a mesh, unless he has some experience in naval affairs. He is unacquainted with the details of the office. He finds men who have become rooted there. Since those bureaus were established, twelve or fourteen years since, they have had a controlling influence. He necessarily looks to them for intelligence; he has to rely on them for information; and after awhile that reliance settles down to submission on his part, and authority on their part over him. Unless a man has a master-will and unbounded capacity to eviscerate a subject, and a will to control and manage it, he will inevitably yield to their machinations, and will feel himself bound in the meshes by which he is surrounded, and at last must yield himself a victim to the designs of packed conspiracies.

Mr. President, we are told that by the action of the board the inefficient alone were to be removed. Does not every one of us know that the inefficient have not been removed; that men of great efficiency have been removed: that men of spotless reputations and high honor have been removed; that men of skill in seamanship have been removed, and their characters stained? We know that others have been retained who were characterized as a portion of the "dry-rot," instead of cutting that off, or separating it from the pure material. That has been the effect. It was efficiency that was required; and yet men are retained in the service who are not efficient—even one of the board himself had his leg broken twice, and Lieutenant Maury had a leg broken only once.

Mr. MALLORY. Will the Senator allow me to say a word here?

Mr. HOUSTON. With great pleasure.

Mr. MALLORY. My friend from Texas authorizes me to interpose an explanation at this point very appropriately; for I am very certain that a gentleman who has distinguished himself in everything that ennobles man, will not possibly charge on a member of the board what I can explain to be an error. The honorable Senator alludes to the case of Lieutenant Maury, who had a leg broken, and said a member of the board had his leg broken twice. He brings this example forward, I presume, as matter of complaint that, if one was removed from the active-service list, (and that was the predisposing cause for the removal,) the other should have been removed also.

I desire to make an explanation as to that point. Lieutenant Missroon, in the active discharge of his duty at sea, had the misfortune of having his leg broken. It was immediately set while he was at sea; and upon it he did two years' sea duty; but finding that he would fail, and being devoted to his profession, what did he do? He left no stone unturned until he found surgeons willing to break it over again. After two years he found surgeons in the United States (having threatened to go to France to find them) who were willing to perform the operation. He did submit to a most painful operation; he had his leg broken over again and reset; and on that leg he has since performed seven years' sea duty. That is the explanation; and I hope the Senator from Texas will not bring up that case to tell against Captain Missroon.

Mr. HOUSTON. Mr. President, I am always very glad to hear the gentleman when he speaks; but I do not see that his explanation has any particular relevancy to this matter. It is true that some days since it was stated in discussion that Mr. Maury had received the injury of a fractured limb. It was rather intimated that this was the cause for disrating him, because otherwise his reputation was spotless. He had performed as fair a proportion of sea duty, during the time he was in the service, as the chairman of the board, and more than several other members of the board. There could have been no objection to him on this ground. His moral standing none can impeach—none dare do it. Then what was the reason for his displacement? I presume there must have been some cause. Because he limps? If that was the only cause for removing him, pray has he not performed duty since his leg was broken? I believe he has. Why has he not performed sea duty for the last seven years? Because it was refused to him when he applied for the privilege of performing it. That is the reason of it; and I desire to have it fairly understood. They must have had some pretext for it. He has performed as fair a proportion of sea duty as the average of officers on the board, and his attainments otherwise are higher. He was like the tall poplar, and must be cut down. He was not only a sailor and a gentleman, but he was a man of science, renowned throughout the world, distinguished by honors which no other citizen had. For this he must be separated from the Navy, and degraded. "Oh!" say the board, "we must be the *élite;* if we get but one whistle, we will take that. That will do some good. We will trumpet you—you will whistle us; and if you do not, you must take care, Thorburn. We will strike you down in a whistle."

I could speak of numbers of others. Take the case of Commander Shaw—one of the best looking men I see about Washington. He looks as though he could himself alone give a broadside to a seventy-four as quickly as it would have been done by Captain Stribling with his undrilled crew. I would just as soon take a chance with him as I would with Stribling, because the inspection showed that before Stribling could bring his guns into action, his vessel might be sunk. Shaw would at least have had two cracks at the enemy before they got nearer. He had an important command in the West Indies at the time; and he was stricken down—for what? Inefficiency? Of course they could not retire him for anything else than inefficiency!

Ringgold, too, one of the most accomplished and scientific officers in the naval service of this or any other country, was also stricken down; and here is Rolando—it is a great mercy he has not been dropped. I should like to know what trumpeting and whistling ought to be done when Rolando shows himself in the streets of Washington city, when marching one hundred men two miles up the beach, and down again, requires a whistle. Sir, a thousand guns for Rolando would be too little a greeting on his return to the American shores. But how did he return? With humiliation, shame, and confusion. He is a man who has acquired for your country a fame which no other man in modern times has done. Sir, his conduct in the China seas is without a parallel. You may take your Nelsons and all the heroes of antiquity; but it will require old Neptune himself to rival Rolando. He has performed feats which electrified the British Navy. Sir, they struck Europe to the heart. They aroused their sluggish impulses, and animated their pride in the recollection, I presume, of former days. The Queen of Spain conferred on him the order of knighthood. What else was done? The English did not participate in the bloody scenes, where the scuppers of his gallant ship gushed blood. When the enemy were forced to run away, they exploded the vessel and threw him into the ocean, but he recovered again. Those who only contemplated his feats of gallantry and chivalry—what was done for them? The captain who commanded the British vessel was made an admiral, and his lieutenant a commodore. What have we done for Rolando? We have disgraced that gallant and chivalrous man. And do you expect glory and honor to perch on the banners of your Navy, and to maintain its well-earned renown, when you strike down such men as Rolando, and leave such men as composed this board? Are you going to confide the honor of the nation to men, regardless of the chivalry of their fellows, who have lost all *esprit du corps*, and who appropriate all favor, all power, all patronage to themselves. Sir, I am not prepared to do it.

These men have had no hearing. The law said their cases should be "carefully" examined. Has the President examined them? No. In the first place the board were to retire those who were inefficient, and drop those morally unworthy. They have done neither, and therefore they have not executed the law. The President has not carefully examined it, and therefore the action is a nullity. He has not exercised the prerogative of the Executive, because he said he acted in accordance with the law; and, in conformity with the law, the officers that are dropped were notified of it, and the words "according to the law" are inserted in his prefatory remarks in the notification to them. Then, it was not by virtue of the prerogative of the executive that it was done.

My friend from Delaware spoke the other day of what General Jackson would have done. Sir, Jackson was incapable of doing anything that did not become a man—a whole man; for he himself was every inch a king. He was nature's king. He was by birth nobility. He was not a king hereditary, but to nature's lineage. Think you, sir, that he would see honorable men stricken down, dishonored, degraded, and humiliated, and others forming combinations to sustain them, trying to subsidize influence, denouncing men through their friends, because they did not come to the support of their bill? No, sir; General Jackson would never do such a thing; but he would, with his own hands, have wiped out forever from the Register the names of those who sat on that board. And I never will, while I live, support any man for power or place who would not revise that board, and exercise his prerogative on those of them who are not able to vindicate themselves against the machinations which stand charged against them by the facts arrayed. We should relieve the public from the odium of the responsibility that must rest on us as a nation, unless we redress it. It can be done, and the Secretary of the Navy has distinctly said so.

Mr. President, there was no necessity for any modification of the laws in relation to the Navy, either as to its government or as to its organization. It was only necessary to make provision for a retired list. All the power necessary for its correction, and for purging it of any improper material, was already in the hands of the executive, either by the Constitution or by the laws. It was in the power of the Secretary of the Navy to order a court of inquiry, in relation to the conduct of any officer; they would report the facts to him and he would submit them to the President, who might then exercise his prerogative. If he lacked the courage to do it, he should report them to the Senate, and ask for their advice and consent in regard to the exercise of his prerogative. After you had provided a retired list for those pronounced incompetent by a board of surgeons, the Navy would be relieved. Thus all the useless portions would be dispensed with, and this remedy would be efficient.

But men have been retired whose positions were proud and preëminent. By these combinations they are stricken down. One instance, to which I have already alluded, is that of Ringgold, one of the *élite* of the Navy, a gallant and chivalrous officer, a most accomplished and skillful seaman, and an elegant gentleman. He, too, has been hopelessly stricken down, because, on one occasion, in the East Indies, when laboring under the miserable effects of quinine, he became delirious and a little errant in mind. Although he recovered from this, it furnished a pretext for striking him down, because he was more gallant, more accomplished, than those who judged him.

The temptation to the officers who served upon the board was too strong for human nature to resist. They were directly interested in the result. The Secretary of the Navy has endeavored to sustain their action by drawing examples from the Army. He urges, as an analogous case, that the Army was reduced under Mr. Madison, and that that was the origin of the system which has arisen. Why, sir, there is no more analogy between the two cases than there is between a common window and a sky-light in form and appearance. After the war of 1812, when all were prepared to be disbanded, Mr. Madison selected three generals, whom he determined to retain in the Army of the United States, and constituted them a board to regulate and prune the Army, exercising their judgment in retaining and removing. In no other respect is there any analogy between that proceeding and this of the naval board. They could not by their action be promoted; but how is it in this case? Strange to say, the gentlemen of the board were directly interested in its results. On this subject Commodore Stewart has said something which is worthy of notice and remembrance. He speaks as a man of sense and experience. He delineates this subject in graphic and striking characters, that must convince every candid man who will impartially review the subject, that he has thoroughly examined it, and that he has examined his own heart—the heart of a soldier, a sailor, a gentleman. From his investigation he came to the conclusion that it was unsafe to intrust to officers even the subject of promotion alone. The board of which he was summoned as a member, and on which he refused to serve, was called to recommend the propriety of promoting, not by seniority, but by selection. He voted against it. He wished to sit with open doors; so did Commodore Jones and others; but we find that the president of the naval board was then in favor of closed doors, and that was effected on this occasion; but Commodore Stewart protested against any such proceeding at the time to which I have alluded. He always voted in the negative upon their action, and it failed. It was under the administration of Mr. Bancroft, Secretary of the Navy.

The protest of Commodore Stewart, is as follows:

Solemn Declaration and Protest of Commodore STEWART, *against the proceedings of a Board of Naval Officers assembled at Washington, on July* 21, 1846.

The honorable Secretary of the Navy, in a communication to me, dated July 11, 1846, directed me to repair to Washington, "to enable the Department to avail itself of the advice of officers of experience."

On the assembling of the convention of officers on the 21st instant, he addressed a communication to us individually and collectively, requiring us to "express your (our) opinion, whether in your (our) judgment, promotions in the Navy should be made with exclusive reference to seniority," &c.

On considering the form and language of these communications, it was evident to me that the Secretary of the Navy required our individual opinions in regard to the matters submitted to us in his communication of the 21st instant. Fully impressed with this conviction, I suggested to this convention, that each officer present should be required to give his individual opinion on all matters then before it; which proposition this convention did not accede to, but proceeded to constitute itself a board or tribunal, wherein the voices of the minority should be stifled, and the vote of the majority of the officers assembled should decide all questions that were to be acted upon by it.

If anything were wanting to render this proceeding on the part of the board more objectionable, it may be found in the fact that the efforts that were made to defeat it were not in some cases considered, and in no case were they placed on the record; and nowhere is there to be found an indication of the opinion or vote of a single member on the subject.

That this course was not in conformity with the views or wishes of the honorable Secretary of the Navy, is made manifest by a reference to his subsequent communication on other matters submitted for our opinions, wherein I am addressed singly as the presiding officer of the board, and in language which required me to express our joint opinion expressly as a board.

Had the honorable Secretary so required our joint opinions on the matter first submitted to us, he would have expressed himself equally explicit. His requirements, then, as communicated to us in his letter of the 21st instant, not having been complied with, I feel it my duty to meet them, so far as it shall lie in my power, and after the manner which to me shall seem most proper.

"*No board of officers, however pure, is competent to pass upon the professional and moral qualifications of any officer, whether for promotion or for any other purpose, unless under all the solemn obligations of oath to do justice—a close and steady investigation into whatever demerits may be alleged, aided by all the lights of testimony in his behalf as well as against him, and a patient hearing of whatever he may have to advance in extenuation or defense.*"

Our naval organization is such that it is hardly possible that the officers composing a board could have much personal knowledge of the qualifications or disqualifications of those whose claims for promotion are to be considered. To illustrate this remark, I will state that, of the fifteen officers whose names have been passed upon by this board, I have no personal knowledge of the qualifications of more than two of them, although I have numbered more than forty-eight years of service, twenty-three of which have been passed at sea. Most of them were unknown to me even by name; and as the remainder of the officers composing this board average a sea service of but eighteen and a half years, it is highly probable that a majority of the board never had an opportunity of forming an opinion of them from personal knowledge in any one case. Yet, notwithstanding this, this board, *by a joint and secret ballot*, has recommended the promotion of certain officers, to the injury of others, and that certain other officers should be considered unworthy of promotion altogether.

The adoption of this *joint and secret ballot* has gone far to render the proceedings of this board justly obnoxious. It has assumed for itself the detestible attributes of the Star Chamber. Not recognized by any law, nor under the protection of any law—*without even the obligation of an oath to do justice to the officer on whose claims it has passed, or to the service*—without any evidence of their merits or disqualifications, or without assigning any reason for its opinions, either individually or collectively—it has given condemnatory judgment on the reputations of men long in the service of their country—one of whom is now abroad serving with distinction—emphatically intimating that they shall not be promoted, and thus virtually disgracing them forever in public estimation.*

There is nothing so precious to an officer as his reputation. When arraigned for alleged offenses before a court-martial, he earnestly, and at a great cost, seeks his vindication. He confronts his accusers, he objects to his judges, he offers his witnesses, his explanations of defense, and the truth is sifted. The judges are under oath to decide according to law, the evidence, and their consciences; and after a fair and impartial trial, the punishment, if any, falls upon him sanctioned by law. And yet such punishment by court-martial can rarely surpass in severity, and in its effects, the judgment pronounced by this board—*a board sitting in secret conclave—their victim abroad, and unheard in his defense; without charges against him, without evidence of any kind, acting on suspicion or hearsay;* without personal knowledge of his qualifications, and many of its members perhaps influenced by personal prejudices and

---

*The officer referred to by Commodore Stewart was Commander Henry, of the United States sloop of war Plymouth, who was furloughed by the board.

LEGATION OF THE UNITED STATES,
RIO DE JANEIRO, *December* 26, 1845.

MY DEAR SIR: Since my visit to the Plymouth with His Excellency Hollanda Cavalcanti, Minister and Secretary of State for the Affairs of the Marine of the Imperial Government of Brazil, on Monday, the 22d instant, I have not had the opportunity until now to make the proper and due acknowledgment of the pride I felt, as an American citizen—as a public functionary of my country, and as one ever alive to the improvement and prosperity of our Navy, in the exhibition of the perfectly beautiful and efficient ship under your command. You, your officers, crew, and corvette are enti led to my testimonial, and you shall have it.

For beauty of naval architecture; for order, system, and comfort of internal arrangements; for man-of-war like appearance; for apparent efficiency; for battery, and particularly its preservation; for cleanliness; for space to fight or

enmities. *Before such a tribunal no one would be safe. A clique, or even a single member of a board, might bring irreparable injury upon the prospects of any officer in the service.* Such proceedings, so contrary to all received notions of propriety and public justice, and so opposed to the principles of our government, I, for one, could never countenance or be a party to. No other course was, therefore, left to me, in the various ballots for the selection of officers for promotion, than to mark on every ballot—*I decline to vote.*

In further illustration of this hasty and obnoxious mode of dispatching officers and disposing of their reputations, I will here state that in one case papers were presented from the files of the Department calculated to create prejudice against that officer whose fate was to be passed upon—papers having no claim to the character of evidence in any court of honor or justice—*and yet, at the same time, other papers and testimonials of character, highly favorable to the individual, and designated as such in the synopsis accompanying the case, were never presented to the board.*

Yet so desirous do I find myself to comply, so far as it is within my competence, with the requisitions of the honorable Secretary of the Navy, that I feel it my duty to state explicitly my opinion upon the chief inquiry propounded, on the decision of which rests his subsequent requirements. These, also, I conceive fully responded to in the opinion I have now the honor to give.

The Hon. Secretary's main proposition, upon which depend all others embodied in his letter of the 21st July, 1846, is in the following words:

"You will express your opinion whether, in your judgment, promotion in the Navy should be made with exclusive reference to seniority?"

In obedience to the injunction contained in this paragraph, *I give it as my opinion that promotion should always be made with exclusive reference to seniority,* except where great gallantry before an enemy shall entitle the officer to the exalted distinction of a preference over his peers, or where immediate guilt or incompetence shall be declared to exist by a tribunal *legally and expressly constituted to determine the question.*

CHARLES STEWART, *Presiding Officer.*

WASHINGTON CITY, D. C., *July* 23, 1846.

But, sir, what was the crying necessity for this attempted "improvement" and revision in the Navy? It is the clamor of young officers who are burning for promotion. Is there any wrong done to them by restraining their anxiety, impassioned as it may be? Not at all. When they enter the Navy they know the conditions under which they do so; they know the rules of the service, and the system of promotion through the various grades; thus they have no right to complain if they cannot obtain promotion in the regular course. By adhering to it we are not wronging them; and is their clamor to displace men who have for thirty or forty years relied on the faith of this Government, that, as long as they demean themselves honorably and usefully to the country, they should be sustained by her? Are they to be displaced to give room for the young aspirants—many of them the relations of members of the board—and to give room for members of the board themselves? Is there a solitary officer who served upon the board who was not directly interested in the revision of the Navy Register, and who did not receive promotion as a consequence of his own individual action? More than half, if not two thirds, promoted not only themselves but also their own relations. Can you tell me, in the face of the country, that such proceedings can be honest, when Commodore Stewart was even opposed to the principle (unless in very extraordinary cases) of going out of the ordinary rule of promotion by rotation.

But here we see men's heads were cut off for the sake of young aspirants and gentlemen who clamor—men who call themselves "the country," "the wisdom of Congress," having all the knowledge of everything that is necessary in order to a revision of the Navy to give efficiency to the right arm of the service. Sir, it is a useless arm now; in its present condition it is paralytic.

The nation has now but one arm, and that is the Army of the country; it is that on which she must rely to defend her. You have fine vessels; you intend to build more; but you have not in the Navy the *personnel* that has been culled out and stricken down. Instead of improving the Navy it has been impaired; its strength and efficiency have been lost by what has been done You must raise it by *repeal;* you must give strength to it by REPEAL; you must confirm its strength by REPEAL; for nothing short of that will do it. That is all that will save the country. I care not so much for individuals as for my country's honor and glory. Think you not that a seventy-four gun ship, filled from keel to deck with Maurys, would not produce in the sailor's heart one single thrill, one glorious aspiration for imperishable renown? If not, then, sir, a thousand retiring boards, filling creation, would never glorify one banner on the bosom of the Atlantic or the Pacific, when they carry with them such principles as their actions have revealed. If they have before sustained a character for bravery, when they come to review their acts they must think "conscience makes cowards of us all." For my deductions I take history, and the official records of the Department for my guide; and I present them to the world with my views upon them, imperfect as they are.

I have referred to the case of Commodore Stewart. That gallant man, a man far above reproach, has felt the iron in his soul inflicted by tyro hands, though he had won renown and glory for his country, dignified its banner, and borne aloft its pennant in victory, when those by whose action he has suffered never saw the enemy—save that one to whom I have already referred—the one of whom I mentioned the whistling. Perhaps one of them was on somebody else's ship, and staid on it, and was shot at, and did his duty; but Stewart did more than his duty. His duty was to defend his country; but he gave it glory in return for its reliance that he would defend it. He was one who gave *prestige* to your Navy, as did Jones, and other illustrious men, who, after having been drenched with blood, and left with mutilated limbs, are now "crushed out"—I use a court phrase—"crushed out." Sir, I do not care to "crush out" others, but I wish to replace those who have been unjustly deprived of their posi-

work; for ventilation by ports or pumps; for adaptation, especially, in all respects to a warm climate; for total absence of all "gimcrackery;" for lightness and yet strength; for elegance without one extravagant or useless ornament; for quiet discipline, and for the sweet and cordial shipshape entertainment which makes so favorable an impression of our country upon strangers abroad, I have never seen a ship of our own or any other nation to surpass, and in some essential respects to equal, the game-looking Plymouth.

His Excellency, the Minister of Marine, who has a good eye, looked inquiringly about him; and was so struck with admiration at the naval model he was inspecting, that he will doubtless seek of you further information to enable him to cause its imitation by the service of which he is the distinguished head.

I trust you will furnish him with drafts, if required; and I have the honor to be, with thanks for the honor you have done our national character, your obedient servant,

HENRY A. WISE.

To Captain HENRY HENRY, *United States ship Plymouth, harbor of Rio de Janeiro.*

tion, and to put them where they ought to stand. I wish to restore the national honor—to redeem its faith that was plighted to them. I desire to wipe out what was imperfectly done, or was rendered a nullity by the want of fidelity in the officers who undertook a proceeding in which partiality and selfishness are their only recommendations.

www.ingramcontent.com/pod-product-compliance
Lightning Source LLC
LaVergne TN
LVHW011144110826
845150LV00008B/2502

9781418192150